CANCEL CULTURE
DICTIONARY

AN A TO Z GUIDE TO
WINNING THE WAR ON FUN

CANCEL CULTURE DICTIONARY

Jimmy Failla

FOX
NEWS
books

HarperCollins books may be purchased for educational, business, or sales promotional use. For information, please email the Special Markets Department at SPsales@harpercollins.com.

Fox News Books imprint and logo are trademarks of Fox News Network, LLC.

FIRST EDITION

Alphabet art by FontStocker/Shutterstock, Inc.; Canceled art by Aguir/ Shutterstock, Inc.

Library of Congress Cataloging-in-Publication Data
Names: Failla, Jimmy, author.
Title: Cancel culture dictionary: an a-to-z guide to winning the war on fun / Jimmy Failla.
Description: First edition. | New York, NY: Broadside [2024] | Includes index.
Identifiers: LCCN 2023043064 (print) | LCCN 2023043065 (ebook) | ISBN 9780063325685 (hardcover) | ISBN 9780063325708 (ebook)
Subjects: LCSH: Cancel culture. | Public opinion. | Social distance. | Social influence.
Classification: LCC HM1176 .F35 2024 (print) | LCC HM1176 (ebook) | DDC 302.23/1—dc23/eng/20231011
LC record available at https://lccn.loc.gov/2023043064
LC ebook record available at https://lccn.loc.gov/2023043065

23 24 25 26 27 LBC 5 4 3 2 1

For my wife, Jenny, and my son, Lincoln.
No man alive has a better two tax write-offs.

Greetings . . . XI

Greetings

Welcome to the big book of cancel culture. The fact that you're even here is a good sign for both of us because it means we haven't been canceled in recent weeks. After all, if I had just fouled out in the big game of life, I don't think they'd be releasing this fancy-pants book with my disgraced name splashed all over it. And if you'd just lost your job, I don't think you'd be out spending money on books.

Unless you suffered a high-powered, fall-from-grace, sex-scandal type of cancel where you left town with a few million bucks and a juicy story about your Red-Hot Naughty Nurse of a Mistress. If that's the case, please hit me up, because I'd love to write a book about you. No hard feelings if you've already got another author on the story, but it goes without saying that I'd still appreciate an introduction to that Naughty Nurse.

I kid! For those of you under the age of forty, "kidding" was something we did just to be funny and nobody cared how it went when I was growing up in the 1980s.

It was a simpler time when Reagan was president and fun was legal. Nobody took life seriously, which was evidenced by the fact that half our outfits contained shoulder pads. The girls had teased bangs and the boys had this thing called masculinity. But you couldn't always tell because a lot of the most popular male rock singers had teased bangs too. Over in the comedy world, Eddie Murphy was telling all kinds of naughty jokes on *SNL* without any fear of blowback. Madonna was doing all kinds of filthy things (and people) on MTV. Hollywood didn't take offense; they took a number. And throughout all of this decadent debauchery, the only one who spent all day obsessing about their phone was E.T.

Yeah, the '80s were famous for an alien who wanted to *phone home*, but the thing that truly sets them apart now was that kids would *leave home*. As in: they went outside to play with other kids, in person, unsupervised, with no app-based tracking device and zero requirements to check in every thirty minutes. As crazy as it sounds in today's world where we geotag our kids twenty-four hours a day like they're federal criminals out on bail, I grew up in a time when our parents *rarely* knew where we were, and neither did we.

We simply went outside, found some fun, and followed it in whatever direction the good times took us "until the streetlights came on." At which point we'd hightail it home to tell everybody about the exotic things we discovered on our voyages. Picture Marco Polo, if he traveled by bicycle and wore a *Ghostbusters* T-shirt.

Giving your kid that type of freedom today would qualify as child neglect in the eyes of the law. And it would certainly lead to a conviction in the court of public opinion, where we're all one bad headline away from mobilizing an online rage mob that knows nothing about you, save for the fact that they want to destroy your existence in the name of getting *likes* and showing the world they know better.

That's cancel culture in a nutshell.

A collection of people who wake up every day looking for something to get offended by so they can leverage their victimhood into your firing and their clout. The trend has become so prevalent in society that scientists have a word for people who do this: they're called *losers*.

Let's face it. You're never going to be at a party and say to your bud-dies, "I can't wait until the guy who gets offended by everything shows up!" And if you do want to hang out with the guy who gets offended by everything, you're out of luck because he doesn't get invited to par-ties.

This book is a collection of people and products that were whacked by the outrage mob for a multitude of reasons big and small. It's not actually a dictionary per se. If anything, the publishers arranged it in *A*-to-*Z* form because, after reading some of my writing samples, they weren't entirely sure I'd ever learned the alphabet to begin with.

I don't know that for a fact, but I can confirm that nobody likes can-cel culture—nowhere in pop culture and not in either political party. But as you'll see in the pages of this book, Republicans and Democrats have gone along with "cancels" over the years. Sometimes they rode that wave because it was helpful to their mission, other times because they didn't want to disagree with the outrage mob and see their own careers die in a hail of tweets. This same logic is what ultimately drives executives at major corporations to give the mob what it wants by fir-ing a celebrity.

The menacing, omnipotent nature of social media storm clouds makes execs feel like it's a cancel-or-be-canceled world. (I was gonna call it a dog-eat-dog world but I'm a little sensitive to the idea of dog meat because I just ate a "chicken" kebob in Times Square.) The point is ex-ecutives sometimes think that firing a celebrity will save their own ass.

But cancels aren't confined to stars and politicians. You'll also come to see that they've consumed careers in every field, from zoo work-ers who trashed their visitors on Facebook to security workers who posted their farts on Instagram. (I'll wait right here while you look up his videos.)

Don't get me wrong: some cancels were necessary and even good for society. (Talking to you, R. Kelly.) But the vast majority of people whose careers were sentenced to death by digital firing squad lost it all for crimes that should have resulted in a much lighter penalty—if any penalty at all. Alas, they were on the wrong side of the keyboard cops in a slow news cycle, so away they went.

The good news is some of the people who get canceled come back. The bad news is some of the people who get canceled come back. And if you don't believe me, you haven't seen Kathy Griffin's latest stand-up act.

Kathy was famously canceled at the beginning of the Trump administration after she posted a picture with a plastic head in it. But enough about *her* face.

If I have one goal for this book, it's to make sure you enjoy it so much, you buy whatever ridiculous book I write next, regardless of how harsh those reviews happen to get.

My second goal is to show you that nothing in our lives has been improved by the era of incentivized outrage. We're more agitated and politically divided, and—despite upending thousands of careers in the name of progress—nobody has anything to show for it beyond the cheap high from the digital dopamine we call "likes."

Which brings me to goal number three: to end this book at a place where we can all agree it's time to stop empowering a movement whose biggest winners are a bunch of losers.

I'm not saying we have to go full 1980s and let the kids run wild in the streets again. But we absolutely need to get back to a time when the world knew the difference between a joke and a hate crime.

Because any society that can't take a joke is destined to become one.

CANCEL CULTURE
DICTIONARY

Awards Shows

Hollywood awards shows used to get incredibly high ratings. But these days the only thing high at the Oscars is Seth Rogen. Heyyo! I've got a million of 'em, people.

There was a time when the Academy Awards had 57 million of 'em, meaning viewers. The year was 1998. *Titanic* took home eleven awards and Leonardo DiCaprio took home at least eleven supermodels. To be clear, I don't have the exact shag numbers from Leo's *Titanic* after-party, but any way you slice it, somebody needs to slow that guy down, or His Heart *Won't Go On.*

Other big winners in '98 included *L.A. Confidential, Good Will Hunting,* and *As Good as It Gets,* which it truly was in terms of ratings.

The 70th Annual Academy Awards was the most-watched Oscars telecast in history, but ever since they honored *Titanic,* celebrities have walked the red carpet while ratings walked the plank. Viewership dipped by 18 percent for the following year's ceremony, with 45 million people tuning in to *The 71st Annual Academy Awards.* History will show that Shakespeare Was in Love, but America had put Oscar in the friend zone, with 12 million fewer views than the previous year's ceremony.

If that weren't bad enough, the Oscars, which is traditionally the second most-watched TV event of the year after the Super Bowl, finished third behind the big game and a Barbara Walters interview with Monica Lewinsky. Every TV insider in America assumed the Oscars would beat the Lewinskys, but in the end, all the Versace gowns in Tinseltown were no match for One Blue Dress in the Oval Office Pantry.

Oscars ratings began to fall because the Academy got away from nominating films that had huge box office success. But Hollywood's programming decisions during the tail end of the Clinton administration didn't hurt half as much as the political rage room that ensued after Donald Trump's election win.

Let's start here:

There's no denying the fact that Trump's victory was a *yuge* upset, and not just in Hollywood but everywhere on earth. Oddsmakers installed Hillary Clinton as the overwhelming favorite to become our first female president, and—backed by the entirety of the media and just about every corner of pop culture—the People's Pantsuit seemed certain to follow her husband into the White House. But in the end, as Bill Clinton might say, when it comes to the presidency, she was close but no cigar.

Was this an emotional loss for tens of millions of people? Yes. But it's worth noting that half the country was thrilled by Trump's victory, yet Hollywood made a conscious effort to alienate every last one of them.

Saturday Night Live used its first cold open after Election Night to feature a teary-eyed Kate McKinnon, dressed as Hillary Clinton, singing Leonard Cohen's spiritual, "Hallelujah." Now, some would say the show had been skipping humor for years, but in this case there wasn't even an attempt. The whole thing was embarrassingly absurd.

Especially when you consider this was the same show that *did* tell jokes in its first cold open after September 11. Yet there was NBC, reacting to the election of a man who had just finished hosting a show *on their network*—for fifteen seasons no less—with more devastation than the biggest terror attack in American history.

Apparently, to NBC, Trump's win was somehow worse than 9/11 because Osama bin Laden never hosted a show called *Celebrity Jihadist*. It's just as well because it would've bombed.

Listen, I don't wanna judge the *SNL* writers' room because those guys get much better drugs than we do. But as a comedian, I've never been more ashamed of our profession, and I say that as someone who's seen Chelsea Handler live twice.

Most comics realize that regardless of what's going on in the world, our job is to make fun of things and bring people together over the shared realities we all face. *SNL* clearly wasn't on the email thread for that one, because the only thing their group therapy session united were viewers and their liquor cabinets. I was gonna add a joke about Hillary drinking, too, but she'd moved on to much stronger stuff than alcohol by then.

Sadly for comedy and America as a whole, the McKinnon Meltdown set the stage for weeks of high-profile Hollywood tantrums that culminated at the Women's March in Washington, which took place a day after Donald Trump's inauguration. The event featured vicious, viral takedowns of the forty-fifth president from the likes of Madonna, Scarlett Johansson, and Ashley Judd. Michael Moore also got in a good rant, and while he's not a woman, they let him onstage anyway because he had some of the biggest breasts at the event.

Unfortunately for Oscars ratings, after two months of watching pampered people in pussy hats scream about the president, most Americans didn't really need to hear any more. Just 30 million viewers tuned in to *The 89th Annual Academy Awards* during Trump's first year in office. It was a far cry from the previous year's 35 million and a much further cry from the all-time high of 57 million in 1998. Emphasis on the word "cry" because the whole show was a well-dressed coping session. If you didn't know any better, you'd think somebody had cut off Hollywood's Xanax supply.

Host Jimmy Kimmel kicked things off by reminding everyone in the room the world hated America because of Trump's election. He followed with more jokes about Trump's Twitter habits and allegations he was racist. From there, it turned into a contest to see who could trash Trump the hardest, with dozens of winners calling out his border policies by insisting, "We should be building bridges and not walls." Of course, after that, they went home to their mansions, which were surrounded by walls.

The hypocrisy wasn't lost on viewers, but the moment was lost on Hollywood, perhaps forever. Just 26 million people tuned in to the following year's ceremony in 2018, the first time viewership plunged below 30 million viewers but not the last, with the final Oscars broadcast of the Trump administration hitting what was then an all-time low of 23 million viewers in 2020. And this was pre-pandemic, so you can't blame Covid. No, the actors were spreading other viruses at the after-parties that night.

The damage done to pop culture by all its Trump tantrums is incalculable, but it wasn't confined to movies. Viewership for the Grammys fell from 25 million during Trump's first year in office to 18 million during his last. The Emmys lost nearly half of all viewership during Trump's term, with viewership sinking from 11.6 million in 2017 to 6 million in 2020.

It's no secret that Hollywood is overwhelmingly liberal, but apparently it's some secret that half of America isn't. Even as we approach the 2024 election, countless celebrities continue to bash conservatives, but the ratings would tell you that liberals are tired too.

Nowhere is that more evident than at the Golden Globes, which not only lost a massive audience during Trump's term but lost the entire 2022 ceremony after he left office, as organizers were forced to *self-cancel* in the wake of another woke protest.

This one started when the *Los Angeles Times* ran an exposé on the Hollywood Foreign Press Association, which handles the nominations for the Globes. According to the *Times*, the HFPA suffered from a lack of diversity in its ranks, and this was to blame for a lack of Black nominations that could only be possible because the group was a bunch of racists.

Now, it's worth pointing out that we were a couple years removed from the Globes handing seven nominations to the nearly all-Black cast of *12 Years a Slave*. You might also mention that the previous year's winners for Best Male Actor and Best Supporting Actor were the late great Chadwick Boseman and the thankfully-still-with-us Daniel Kaluuya, both of whom were Black. There had been dozens of Black winners in major categories over the previous decade, meaning the Globes had hardly declared war on minorities. But once that outrage wave began to rise, every prominent actor in Hollywood jumped on a surfboard.

Scarlett Johansson started by telling *Entertainment Weekly* not only that the HFPA was racist but that they had asked her sexist questions in the past too. A day after the *Black Widow* beatdown, Tom Cruise landed Maverick's F-14 and announced he was giving back all three of his Golden Globes due to the lack of inclusion at the HFPA. I'm sure he also resented the trophies because they were taller than him, but that part never made it into the statement. The point is, once Cruise called it quits, that year's broadcast became a Mission Impossible, if you will, and NBC was forced to pull the plug.

I'm not an expert on the Hollywood foreign press, but if the actors really think it's racist and sexist, then it was an honorable stance for them to take. That being said, it definitely wasn't a profitable one, because just 6.3 million people watched the Golden Globes when the ceremony returned to TV in 2023. That was even less than the pandemic-plagued audience of 2021, which drew what was then an all-time low of 6.9 million viewers.

There's just no denying that Hollywood's obsession with politics has ratings falling faster than Joe Biden at a commencement speech. Things will only get worse as they ramp up the inclusion initiatives, which the Oscars plans to do by rolling out entirely new nominating criteria at the 2024 ceremony.

Dig this: in order for a film to be eligible for Best Picture at the 96th Academy Awards, at least 30 percent of the film's cast must be a member of an underrepresented group, such as women, the LGBTQIA+ community, people with physical disabilities, or a racial group other than white.

You'll notice there's no criteria for being a *good* actor, or having a *great* script, but there is a requirement that *all* Best Picture nominees have a main story line that centers on members of underrepresented communities.

Translation: If *The Godfather* were being made today, the only way it could win Best Picture is if Marlon Brando started identifying as the Godmother and made somebody "an offer he couldn't *hear*." It goes without saying that when Sonny got shot up at the causeway, at least half the mobsters would need to be women of minority descent. And given all their Second Amendment bashing, it's likely the iconic line of "Leave the gun. Take the cannoli" would be shortened to just "Leave the gun." For all we know, the cannoli came from one of those bakeries that doesn't support gay marriage.

Earth to Hollywood: Nobody asked for this, and not because they're against diversity and inclusion, but because our entire existence has been reduced to a constant reminder of the need for diversity and inclusion. It's in everything we do. Sports, video games, grocery stores—there is no way to leave your house and not get trampled in a social justice stampede.

Even if we did want another partisan lecture, we wouldn't want it from a group of people who have their words written for them. I'm not saying that to slight actors; I'm saying it to implore them to stick to doing what they do best, which is cocaine.

Hollywood actors are famous because they hit the genetic lottery. These folks are so good-looking that we're willing to pay $15 for popcorn to watch them recite words that were written by an ugly person. Take it from a guy who's worked in a bunch of writers' rooms. We're not exactly a herd of show ponies.

Actors are. And awards shows used to be a place where we were all okay celebrating just how incredibly blessed these people happened to be. We didn't hate them for being more gifted than us. If anything, we admired them and lived vicariously through their exploits when we read about them in *People* magazine and *Vanity Fair*.

Even when the good times ended in prison time, America has always stuck with actors. If you don't believe me, you've never met Hugh Grant or the hooker he got caught with. Sure, Mr. Grant wound up in handcuffs, but he also wound up in some of the highest-grossing romcoms of all time following his arrest. Robert Downey Jr.'s drug use found him behind a set of iron bars long before he became Iron Man.

The truth is America has stuck with Hollywood through everything you can think of and a lot of things you can't. When awards shows went activist, it was a Bridge on the River Kwai too far, if you will.

For one thing, nobody wants to get a lecture on inequality from an actress who's wearing a dress that costs more than their house. And even when we do agree with the causes, such as we did in the #MeToo movement, it was hard for anyone to take Hollywood seriously, knowing just how many of them looked the other way on decades of Harvey

Weinstein's abuses. Oprah Winfrey may have brought down the house with her famous "Time's Up" speech at the 2017 Golden Globes, but she still hasn't brought down all the photos of her and Harv yucking it up while his predatory behavior was the worst-kept secret in Hollywood. Don't get me wrong, we're all on board with protecting women, but it sounds a little silly coming from an Oscars crowd that once gave a standing ovation to Roman Polanski decades after he fled the country for raping a thirteen-year-old girl.

It's amazing that Hollywood always looks so ready for its close-up, because apparently none of them own a mirror.

People go to the movies because they need an outlet to unplug, but these days Hollywood is a constant reminder to plug in your electric car. The endless activism is failing America because when Hollywood began bashing conservatives, we lost the common culture that holds us together.

Think about it. We used to have places where we could put our political differences aside for a few hours to consume something we all agreed was fun. Late-night comedy, professional sports, and, yes, movies were a way to lower the political temperature and remind people that, despite the ideological differences, our basic needs were all the same.

Sadly, all of those outlets for escapism have gone political in the years since Trump took office, and it's denying Americans a place to coexist. Baseball used to be our national pastime, but today it's been replaced by fighting on social media.

And whereas Hollywood awards shows used to be a place where the whole country could embrace a film like *Titanic*, today these shows are nothing more than a sinking ship.

Note to entertainment outlets everywhere:

If it ain't woke, don't fix it.

Broadcasters

There's an ongoing debate in society over whether speech is violence. As a former New York City cabdriver who's been punched, kicked, and hit with a trumpet while a mariachi band fought in my back seat, I can tell you firsthand that words don't hurt half as much as fists, feet, and flying instruments. What a truly bizarre moment that was. Cabbies are always ready to blow the horn, but nothing prepares us for getting hit by one.

There can be no doubt that speech is violence against your own career if you say the wrong things during a live broadcast or tweet them during some downtime in your hotel.

Nobody knows that better than former Major League pitcher Mike Bacsik, who threw a wild pitch on Twitter and was ultimately fired from a Dallas radio station for comments he made about an NBA playoff game.

Bacsik's first brush with fame came as the pitcher who gave up Barry Bonds's record-breaking 756th career home run in April 2007. There wasn't a dry eye in the house that night, mainly because of the steroids, which have a way of making people emotional. Bacsik went viral a second time for all the wrong reasons in April 2010. The sport in question this time was basketball and Bacsik, who had been appearing regularly on KTCK Radio in Dallas, quickly disappeared after he shot an airball on Twitter. His hometown Dallas Mavericks were in a heated playoff series against their interstate rival, the San Antonio Spurs, when midway through game five the referee made a call that seemed to favor the Spurs.

Bacsik responded on Twitter by saying, *Congratulations to all the dirty Mexicans in San Antonio.*

Times like these make me think social media needs a Breathalyzer device that you blow into before you're allowed to tweet to the whole entire world.

Unfortunately for Bacsik, it doesn't exist yet, and to be clear, I don't know that he's even a drinker. He dang sure tweeted like one, though, and the man who got his start on sports channels was now being shown on CNN—and some news channels as well.

As the tweet was causing all kinds of cable news carnage, he apologized for his comments, claiming they were based in sarcasm that didn't translate with Twitter users. They clearly didn't translate with his radio bosses, either, and Bacsik was suspended indefinitely. The backlash grew so loud that a second statement was issued a day later announcing that he'd been sent on a permanent vacation. I'm not sure where he went, but something tells me it wasn't San Antonio.

Now, was Mike Bacsik some type of a raging racist, as many

claimed? I'd have a hard time issuing that verdict after one profoundly stupid tweet. Regardless, there's no place in society for those types of comments, so it's impossible to defend the guy without ultimately getting yourself canceled along the way.

What I will go to bat for is the need to issue sentencing guidelines in the court of public opinion. Right now, whenever somebody says something dumb, online prosecutors always recommend the career death penalty. Surely there has to be room for a fine or a suspension in certain instances? After all, the practice of losing one's job the first time you say something stupid isn't a great strategy for any of us to endorse in the long run, given how flawed we all happen to be.

Don't get me wrong: there are certain comments that are too far out there even for me. Radio legend Don Imus made one of them in April 2007.

The I-Man, as he was known, looked like he got his start in radio covering the invention of fire. Truth be told, he began his broadcast career in 1964 and built up a massive audience of people who loved his surly style of put-down humor. Whether he was bashing staffers or brutally mocking current events, Imus was a morning host with the cranky demeanor of someone who wasn't a morning person, and audiences loved him for it.

Time magazine had named him one of the 25 Most Influential People in *America*. Not just radio, but the country as a whole. He may have looked like an angry chain-smoking lesbian, but he made enough people happy to become a member of the National Broadcasting Hall of Fame.

None of that mattered on the morning of April 4, 2007, when he was discussing the previous night's NCAA women's championship basketball game. Imus and his staff were watching highlights on camera during the MSNBC simulcast of his CBS radio show when the following exchange ensued between the host and his longtime producer, the late Bernard McGuirk:

IMUS: That's some rough girls from Rutgers. Man, they got tattoos and—

MCGUIRK: Some hard-core hos.

IMUS: That's some nappy-headed hos right there. I'm gonna tell you that now, man, that's some—woo! And the girls from Tennessee, they all look cute, you know, so like, kinda like, I don't know.

They went on to compare the women to a pair of basketball teams in Spike Lee's movie *Do the Right Thing*, but you could barely hear them over the sound of sponsors pulling out of the show. The phrase "nappy-headed hos" was instantly everywhere. All over cable news, just about every newspaper you could think of, and Imus got some extra help from an upstart social media app called *Twitter*, which was a year old at the time.

The good news for Imus was Twitter didn't have nearly the reach it does now. The bad news was it didn't matter. His comments were *everywhere*. It was impossible to change the radio station in my *taxi* that spring and not hear about it on whatever station you tuned in to next.

Every passenger who jumped in had a take, because prior to the smartphone swallowing human interaction whole, taxis were the original social media, with everyone weighing in on the hottest topics of the day, whether you asked them to or not. Even the other cabbies who traditionally honked at red lights as a means of getting your attention so they could make eye contact while they gave you the finger were now rolling up to the intersection, giving the horn a toot, and saying "nappy-headed hos." Although it didn't sound half as offensive in their broken English as it did in Imus's broken person.

He was trending off the charts, and the longer it lasted, the bigger the controversy got. Nearly every high-profile guest and sponsor denounced his comments, and civil rights activists Al Sharpton and Jesse Jackson began leading calls for his dismissal. I'm sure it didn't help that his show frequently impersonated both men as grifters over the years. Long story short, they were both ready to collect some payback, although surprisingly it wasn't coming in cash this time.

Imus publicly apologized to the Rutgers women's team and asked for the right to privately apologize as well. But by then there was no saving him, and CBS pulled the plug on the morning of April 12, 2007. In a cruel twist, the announcement came on Imus's radio platform, halfway through his annual telethon, which had raised over $40 million for children's charities since 1990. That morning's broadcast raised over $1.3 million after Imus opened the show by imploring listeners to donate as much as possible, seeing as it could be their last telethon on the station, which it was.

Imus's firing was our first major collaborative cancel in that it built to a crescendo on multiple platforms until it became too big for his employers to ignore. Believe me, they wanted to wait out the storm, because if they were truly incensed by his comments, it wouldn't have taken eight days to fire him.

This really was one of the very first examples of the cancel crowd moving markets. CBS held the line until they saw the sponsors skip town, at which point there was nothing left to do but pull the plug. If a bigger news story had ensued during the initial window of outrage and taken the I-Man out of the headlines and the heat off his sponsors, there's no doubt he would've survived.

We only know this because less than *eight months* after his cancel was the number one trending story in America, Imus got right back on the air like the whole thing never happened. True story. In November 2007, he signed a deal with WABC Radio that also included a simulcast on Fox Business.

There was no huge backlash. There were no boycotts. By then the cancel crowd had moved on to new causes, proving that it was never about the original one. You see, giving the mob power didn't actually give them values. It simply gave them a license to wreck anyone who stepped out of line.

For that reason, Imus was able to last another twelve years on both platforms, and he never really changed the show in any notable way because he didn't have to. The mob was done with him once they got their way in 2007, so much so that there was hardly a mention of his passing in 2019.

It's hard to say if Imus would've made it back onto the air had he been alive to make the same vile comments today. Calling an entire women's basketball team a bunch of nappy-headed hos is far more delicate these days, especially when you consider that some of them are biological men.

Could you say "nappy-headed hombres" and live to tell the tale? I'm not sure, but the increased presence of social media in our lives has made the glare so much more intense that, at the very least, it would've taken him a lot longer to get back behind the mic.

Regardless of how things went, it wouldn't do much to shorten the list of broadcasters who've been fired for saying dumb things on the air.

National Hockey League announcer Jeremy Roenick was put in the permanent penalty box for joking in February 2020 about having a three-way with his wife and a female co-host. He apologized and said the comments were made in jest, but the outrage mob kept the pressure on NBC, so unfortunately for Roenick, he did not get off. In more ways than one.

Two high school basketball announcers fouled out of a Maine radio station after body-shaming female players in January 2022. I won't get into the specifics of their comments about the shape these girls were in, but I will confess to making similar ones about myself after Thanksgiving dinner. I wish I was kidding, but last holiday season was out of control. You know you've gotten fat when you're out of breath from *reading*.

Major League Baseball announcer Thom Brennaman was fired for failing to read the room, and the microphone settings for that matter, when he slandered the gay community during a commercial break in May 2022.

It's still unclear what city Brennaman was referring to when he made an aside to a colleague about the town being, quote, "one of the f*g capitals of the world." Unfortunately for Brennaman, every capital of the world heard it because his mic was on, and the clip instantly went viral.

In a truly surreal—and now legendary—scene, he was forced to come back from commercial and immediately begin an on-air apology. But the game was also back from commercial. He began, "I made a comment earlier tonight that, uh, I guess, uh, went out over the air that I am deeply ashamed of. Uh, if I have hurt anyone out there, I can't tell you how much I say from the bottom of my heart I'm so very, very sorry. I pride myself and think of myself as a man of faith—as there's a drive into deep left field by Castellanos. It will be a home run. And so that'll make it a 4–nothing ball game. . . ."

So as he was speaking, a player on the Cincinnati Reds belted a home run, and the play-by-play interrupted his apology! When the player concluded his home run trot, Brennaman finished striking out by saying, "I don't know if I'm gonna be putting on this headset again." As of this printing, neither do we. He was fired by the Ohio Sports Network that employed him and hasn't been heard on air since.

North Carolina State University announcer Gary Hahn was slightly more fortunate after he got flagged for unsportsmanlike conduct during a college football game in December 2022. Hahn was calling the Duke's Mayo Bowl between NC State and Maryland when he gave the following scoreboard update on another football game, the Sun Bowl, which was being played in Texas:

"Down amongst all the illegal aliens in El Paso, it's UCLA 14 and Pittsburgh 6."

It's worth noting that at the time of his comments, the Sun Bowl was being forced to cancel its annual Fan Festival because the El Paso Convention Center was being used to hold migrants awaiting immigration proceedings in the courts. Unfortunately for Hahn, his employer decided the migrants weren't the only ones who had crossed a border, and he was suspended.

It happened over the holidays, so the media focus wasn't very big. For that reason Hahn, who'd been named the NCAA's announcer of the year in 2010 and again in 2020, was ultimately brought back after serving a two-week penalty. He remains employed to this day, but there's no guarantee it'll stay that way if the White House doesn't get this migrant crisis under control.

The sports world will only rack up new cancels as the line between politics and entertainment continues to blur. We could argue for days over whether it's good to mix the two. I'm personally against it. Sports should serve as an escape from hard news, but no matter where you stand on the issue, one thing remains clear:

The old adage that "defense wins championships" definitely applies to the media just as much as the players. Especially if you're one of those broadcasters with a strong offensive line.

Cosby, Chappelle, and C.K.

Bill Cosby, Dave Chappelle, and Louis C.K. are three of the most talented comedians of all time. I don't know that they've ever shared a stage, but if it does happen, something tells me Dave and Louis aren't gonna let Cosby bartend in the greenroom.

The one thing they have shared is a "cancel" of sorts. Two of them made it out in one piece. In Cosby's case, he can just be glad he's not in prison anymore, which is nothing to sleep on. But enough about his dating life.

There were always rumors dating back to the 1970s that Cosby had been drugging his female companions. But up until 2018, the story was a classic he-said, she-said . . . she-said, she-said, she-said, she-said, she-said.

All of that changed when Cosby was convicted of assaulting a former Temple University employee named Andrea Constand, who had worked at the school when Cosby took advantage of her in 2004. The case became the tip of the spear in the #MeToo movement, and the conviction coincided with the cancellations of dozens of high-level Hollywood executives like Harvey Weinstein and CBS CEO Leslie Moonves. But whereas Weinstein and Moonves were behind-the-scenes power players, the Cosby cancel was different because of just how huge a star he'd become during the run of his insanely popular sitcom.

The Cosby Show averaged 62 million viewers a week when it debuted on NBC in 1984. To give you some perspective, that's nearly three times as much as a show like *Seinfeld*, which averaged close to 20 million viewers over its run. Even an iconic show like *Friends* "only" averaged 23 million at its peak.

Incidentally, 23 million is also what the rent would be on that massive *Friends* apartment in real life. I know that sounds pricey, but let's not forget, it's New York, so each roommate would also receive their own personal rat and a pantless wino to greet them on the way in and out of the building.

As for the Cosby brownstone, it was home to one of the most popular TV families in American history, and it built on the legacy of *The Jeffersons*, which was a trendsetter in focusing on an upper-middle-class Black family. Predominantly Black sitcoms like *Good Times* and *Sanford and Son* became hits before Cosby, but with apologies to Redd Foxx and Jimmie Walker, it was Cosby who found the true ratings "dy-no-mite."

The man who played Dr. Cliff Huxtable on camera became known as America's Dad off it. His stand-up shows sold out arenas around the world and continued to do so in the decades after his sitcom ended its run on NBC. Cosby also remained one of the most sought-after corporate spokespersons in his TV afterlife, so much so that in 2011 he was abducted into the Advertising Hall of Fame. Sorry, *inducted*. It's so easy to confuse the two with Cosby.

But the point is, yes, I looked it up, and there is such a thing as the Advertising Hall of Fame. I'll tell you about it in a minute, but first, a word from our sponsors.

Unfortunately for Cosby, all of this goodwill melted faster than a Jell-O Pudding Pop in July after a comedian told a story about him that went viral on YouTube.

Hannibal Buress is a star in his own right, having appeared for multiple seasons in *Broad City* and *The Eric Andre Show*. But history will show that his biggest impact on showbiz came in October 2014 when he talked about Dr. Huxtable's malpractice issues in a stand-up set. Video of the story quickly exploded on the internet and sparked a conversation in every corner of social media about the longtime rumors regarding Cosby's nonconsensual love life. Ironically the trend peaked in the worst way possible with some accidental help from Cosby's team the following month.

Dig this: in November 2014, America's Dad was ramping up for a comeback to America's TV screens. He had a stand-up special coming to Netflix and NBC was putting the finishing touches on a *Cosby Show* anniversary special. Like most cancels, it was a "so far, so good" scenario until social media got involved. In this case, the fatal flaw surfaced when NBC's marketing team attempted to draw some eyeballs to the comeback by having the comic tweet a request for memes using the hashtag #CosbyMeme.

They were hoping to drum up some nostalgia heat for the big reunion show, and the good news was they got tens of thousands of memes. The bad news was 90 percent of them depicted Cosby as an ugly-sweater-wearing sexual-assault connoisseur. And, yes, there were more pudding jokes than you can shake a Popsicle stick at.

Now, I didn't work in NBC's marketing department at the time, but I feel pretty confident in saying this was not the reaction they were going for. Within two hours of the post, America's weirdest dancer had become America's Most Wanted with anyone and everyone calling him a serial sexual assaulter. The backlash was so intense that Netflix canceled the comedy special the next morning, and a day later NBC pulled the plug on the reunion show altogether.

Looking back, I'm not sure what's crazier: the fact that he was able to conceal his criminal capers for as long as he did or the fact that it blew sky-high only because a social media campaign backfired.

Regardless, it would be hard to argue that any comic suffered a bigger fall from grace—mainly because no comic ascended to higher heights than the man behind *The Cosby Show* and Fat Albert. Forgive me. In the woke world we're now living in, I believe we have to say Plus-Sized Albert.

At his peak, Cosby was on in just about every house in America. And don't get me wrong: we always thought he belonged in jail for making *Leonard Part 6*. But we didn't expect him to wind up there because he was going from *I Spy* to Spanish fly in the greenroom.

Cosby's quick conviction in the court of public opinion didn't end the fury surrounding his problematic past. More than fifty women came forward in the ensuing months with accusatory tales about the disgraced comic, and it prompted prosecutors to take another look at his creepy case history. That resulted in a conviction in 2018 based on his own testimony in a previous civil case brought by one of his victims, Andrea Constand, which was ultimately overturned on a technicality.

He was sentenced to ten years behind bars, and I think everybody who followed Cosby's story will drink to that. Provided we can mix it ourselves.

Like Cosby, Louis C.K. had his own successful sitcom on FX. But the difference is Louis C.K. got in trouble for being exactly the guy he played on TV.

In the fall of 2017, just weeks after Harvey Weinstein was taken down and the #MeToo movement was in full swing, five women came forward claiming C.K. asked them to watch him engage in a certain solo sex act. Now, I don't want to get too graphic here. Let's just say that Louis may not be Catholic, but he definitely celebrates Palm Sunday.

The women accused C.K. of leveraging the power dynamic in their relationship by asking them to watch his one-man show. Seeing as he was the much bigger-name comic with a high-powered agent, they claimed Louis had made it hard to refuse his C.K. for fear of the effect it might have on their careers.

Society was quick to side with his accusers in the midst of all the #MeToo mayhem, and although C.K. issued a rare apology fully owning the behavior, the fury was so intense that there were no defenders left to stick it out for *him*, some pun intended.

The cancel parade started with Jon Stewart announcing that Louis would no longer be appearing in that week's stand-up charity blowout, *Night of Too Many Stars*. Netflix marched in behind Stewart and announced it would not be releasing Louis's new film, *I Love You, Daddy*, which was scheduled to come out that same week. HBO picked up the baton from there and canceled all reruns of his show *Lucky Louie*. And just like that, the most successful comedian of the 2010s had become the first person to get #MeToo'd for sexually assaulting himself.

To be clear, Louis's behavior was disgusting. That being said, I'm not gonna sit here and shame the guy all these years later because the amount of shame you must feel to ask a woman to watch you "shake hands with the governor" is a lot harsher than anything we can throw at him anyway.

Society seemed to agree that he'd paid his debt on this one because, two years after his cancel, C.K. began performing in comedy clubs again and regained his status as one of the top touring acts in the country. He won a Grammy for the Best Comedy Album of 2022. He also sold out Madison Square Garden in the fall of 2023, so I think it's safe to say that Louis lived to tell the tale. Let's just hope he's not breathing too heavily if he tells it over the phone.

Like Louis and Cosby before him, Dave Chappelle also had his own massively successful TV show, but he was never accused of doing anything to women. No, Dave's troubles started when he began making jokes about women who used to be men.

The man who gave the world *Chappelle's Show* on Comedy Central made huge headlines in 2019 when he signed a deal with Netflix to produce four stand-up specials for what was believed to be $100 million. It sounds like a lot, but after taxes . . .

The hullabaloo got a lot heavier when his first special, *Dave Chappelle: Sticks & Stones*, trashed the rampant cancel culture sweeping the country. He also challenged some of the claims made in the Michael Jackson documentary *Leaving Neverland*, and those jokes definitely rubbed a lot of people the wrong way. (Chappelle controversially claimed Michael never rubbed anyone any which way.)

Chappelle's theme for *Sticks & Stones*, which took place at the absolute height of the #MeToo movement, was that America was living in *Celebrity Hunting Season*. He opened by declaring that he loathed a culture that had become consumed with digging up old dirt in order to ruin people's careers. Seriously, somebody could write a book about that. He joked about how incentivizing people to go looking for things to get upset about also teaches them to lose their handle on the difference between words and deeds, hence the title. It was a hilarious special, but some members of the trans community didn't like Dave's jokes about how they were changing the language to accommodate pronouns. To be clear, when I say *they* were changing the language I mean a group of people and not a singular person, which it also now means.

Toward the end of the special, Chappelle told a story about how he was talking to a trans friend and didn't want to offend the person, so he started the conversation by saying "Hello, whatever pronoun you call yourself." The bit inspired hundreds of think pieces condemning the comic for punching down and making a mockery of trans culture. Social media even chimed in with trending hashtags calling on Netflix to #CancelChappelle, but the joke was on them.

Not only did he refuse to apologize, but Netflix ignored calls to pull the special, and *Sticks & Stones* went on to win the Grammy Award for Best Comedy Album in 2020.

Chappelle 1, Outrage Mob 0.

This was the first step in exposing the outrage mob's fatal flaw: they have nothing other than social pressure. If more companies and people stand their ground like Netflix and Chappelle, the mob eventually moves on because there's nothing else they can do but tweet. Sure, they'll protest and boycott for a day or two, but when it comes to comedy, most people have enough things to deal with in life that they don't have the luxury of consuming themselves with a joke that was told at a show they didn't even attend.

I mean, really think about how privileged you have to be to make Netflix comedy specials the object of your ire. First of all, these specials are behind a paywall, and they are viewed *on demand*, which means you only watched after you *demanded* to see it. Second of all, we have zero data correlating jokes with violence because—here's a news flash—the people who can laugh at things aren't usually the ones who snap and go crazy. It's the people who are wound too tight who ultimately go off the deep end. So if you're really looking to protect people, maybe we should *defund the joke police* and teach people to laugh at themselves, which is one of the most valuable life skills anyone can ever develop.

Despite the massive success of *Sticks & Stones*, the joke police stayed on the cancel case, mainly because they had nowhere else to go. Trust me: nobody wants to party with people who freak out over *laughter*. It's one of the purest joys we'll ever know! What's next? Do you protest puppies? Slash the tires on the ice cream truck? Seriously, these angry elves need to make like Princess Elsa and Let It Go. Yes, I quoted a Disney film. No, I didn't see it in the theater because most of my opening acts aren't allowed within five hundred feet of that many kids. But the fact remains, people need to get over themselves. And Chappelle proved it when his follow-up special, *Dave Chappelle: The Closer*, was released on Netflix in 2021.

Once again, Dave opened by taking aim at his usual targets in pop culture and politics, but from there he revisited his dicey relationship with the trans community, at which point the war drums began to beat on Twitter.

This time around, Dave poked fun at them for being too sensitive about his jokes and defended his position, saying, "Gender is a fact. Every human being in this room, every human being on earth, had to pass through the legs of a woman to be on earth."

Dave may have given the correct answer on a biology exam, but you never let the truth get in the way of a good protest, and the outrage mob wasn't about to start now. Within hours of the special's release, the Twitter firing squad was loading up their digital muskets and getting ready to put a blindfold over his career.

Netflix was hit with company-wide protests from its staff in the ensuing days as #CancelChappelle trended on Twitter once again. Multiple walkouts took place at its headquarters in Los Gatos, California, over the next week, with hundreds of employees vowing to quit altogether if leadership didn't pull the special from the service.

I'm not sure how anybody expected this one to play out but, to its credit, Netflix corporate leadership took a public stance that showed more balls than a women's swimming meet. With the backlash swirling in every hallway of its headquarters, management issued an internal memo to employees expressing its support for Chappelle.

It was titled "Netflix Culture—Seeking Excellence" and made it clear that "as employees we support the principle that Netflix offers a diversity of stories, even if we find some titles counter to our own personal values. Depending on your role, you may need to work on titles you perceive to be harmful. If you'd find it hard to support our content breadth, Netflix may not be the best place for you."

Translation: Jokes are not hate crimes, and if you don't know the difference, the door is that way.

Chappelle 2, Outrage Mob 0.

Few things have made me happier in my comedy career than seeing Netflix stare down the mob because it was truly a win for everyone, including supposedly marginalized groups.

Here's the thing: what all these inclusion freedom fighters need to realize is that there's no higher form of inclusion than being made fun of by a comedian. In that moment, we are treating you as an equal who can laugh at themselves just like every other group in the room. True equality does not come by seating one group off at the kiddie table, like some kind of infantilized lesser-than who's off-limits.

No, equality comes when everybody at the show is in the splash zone. Black, white, Muslim, Asian, Indian, Latino, gay, straight, male, female, trans, elderly, handicapped—even folks with dementia—can be made fun of. Although, to be fair, you don't see a lot of people with dementia in comedy clubs. These days they keep them in the Oval Office.

The reason more comics like Chappelle are standing their ground is they know that comedy cancellations have always been a tyranny of the minority. Ninety-nine percent of the people who consume stand-up do so because they're looking for an escape from the torments of everyday life. They don't pay a cover charge and a two-drink minimum to ruin the guy providing that outlet.

Jokes were never meant to be treated like calls to action. Comedy is simply supposed to be treated like a buffet: if you see a joke you like, you throw it on your tray. If you don't like a joke, there's no need to get upset and hold up the line. Just keep walking, because everyone gets their own tray. Take what you want and leave what you don't.

Think about it. If you went to a buffet that served boneless spareribs and you didn't like boneless spareribs, you wouldn't inconvenience the whole entire restaurant by screaming at the chef for his decision to put them on the menu in the first place. And if you would, then congratulations on being the kind of self-important jackass who belongs in the cancel crowd.

To its credit, Netflix realizes you can't run a multibillion-dollar company by catering to every grievance in the break room, especially when some of those grievances are so divorced from reality.

I say that because Dave has gone on to sell hundreds of thousands of tickets around the world, and—despite dire warnings from his critics—nobody has been killed by these jokes or inspired to kill anyone else.

There's an old saying that "laughter is the best medicine." I don't know if that's entirely true, but if we've learned anything from this chapter, it's definitely better than anything Dr. Huxtable was prescribing. Which is why we should defund the joke police and go looking for the real criminals.

Dr. Seuss, Roald Dahl, and The Dukes of Hazzard

Dr. Seuss's first book was rejected twenty-seven times before it was finally published. But if you think that's a lot of rejections, you didn't see me at the bar in my twenties. It probably didn't help that I had the same hairstyle as the Lorax. But let's just say that if Seuss devoted a book to me asking out women, it would be called *Horton Hears a "NO!"*

As for the good doctor, he wasn't one. Theodor Seuss Geisel added the title while he was in college at Dartmouth because he thought it would appease his father, who wanted him to study medicine. He also hoped it would give his writing more credibility with readers, and it seems to have worked. Seuss's books went on to sell over 600 million copies, and they were translated into twenty different languages, including difficult dialects like New Jersey. Which explains the title *Da Cat in da Hat*.

But not even the best-selling children's author of all time could outrun cancel culture, even if it did take nearly thirty years after his death for it to catch up with him.

There's no doubt Dr. Seuss's books would be different if they were published today. For starters, they'd probably avoid controversy by changing *Green Eggs and Ham* to *Cage-Free Eggs and Impossible Ham*. And he'd likely play it safe with *Oh, the Places You'll Go as Long as You've Been Vaccinated!*

However, it wasn't the titles that got Seuss canceled in the afterlife, nor was it the fact that he was faking his status as a doctor. No, the outrage mob gave him a pass on that one, thinking that if they're okay with letting Elizabeth Warren pretend to be Native American in the Senate, then it's okay to let a dude play doctor in the library.

What is not okay for a dude to do is draw illustrations of Black people by the crass and cartoonish standards of 1937. You might point out that society had different attitudes back then, but you didn't stand to lose a gazillion bucks if today's society disagreed with you.

His publishers did, and in March 2021, Dr. Seuss Enterprises announced it would no longer publish six of Seuss's books because of imagery the company deemed to be "racist and insensitive." The list included his very first title, *And to Think That I Saw It on Mulberry Street*, as well as the iconic *If I Ran the Zoo*.

You might call this a preemptive cancel, in that the company wasn't facing a backlash so much as it was filled with recent liberal arts grads who were, like, *ew. no.*

So they took the same adventure that many grievance tourists before them had taken in pulling books like *To Kill a Mockingbird* and *Gone with the Wind* off the shelves in parts of the country because of the problematic language from the era they were written in. But as heinous as we might find the words today, the author's biggest offense at the time was not owning a time machine.

After all, they had no way of knowing how the rules would change eighty years later, which is why it's not practical to hold anyone to standards that didn't exist when their works were released.

I also don't think it's good for society to banish books with problematic language because, in a lot of ways, these books represent the progress we've made on the issue. You know the whole line about people who don't learn from their past being condemned to repeat it? It doesn't appear that anybody on the book canceling board heard it, because the company released a statement saying that "ceasing sales of these books is only part of our commitment and our broader plan to ensure Dr. Seuss' catalog represents and supports all communities and families."

Translation: Nobody said anything about these books, but it's better to self-cancel six of our titles than it is to risk someone sparking a backlash against all of them. The last thing we want is a visit from the Grinch Who Stole Royalties.

Of course, no performative good deed goes unpunished in the land of misfit toys we call social media, so their attempt to avoid controversy wound up starting an even bigger one that divided the country.

Liberals were seemingly pro-cancel and took an understandably hostile stance toward Seuss's earliest drawings. Conservatives saw it as another manufactured controversy by the grievance-minded left—after all, it's not like kids read these books for their faithful depiction of the real world—and accused the Dr. Seuss Enterprises board members of selling out to the woke mafia.

Then House minority leader Kevin McCarthy posted a video that showed him reading *Green Eggs and Ham* and voicing his support for the late author. Thousands of other conservatives joined him on the front lines of the latest culture war, firing out every meme and snarky Seuss tweet they could get their hands on.

The bad news for the publishers is the company was pounded all over social media, and they took plenty of shots from guys like me on cable news too. The good news is that the backlash turned out to be immensely profitable, thanks to conservatives who ran out and bought the books as a middle finger to the liberals. And so began the era of the protest purchase, where one side of the aisle began buying products to signify their opposition to the other side. It's not always enough to help a brand's bottom line, which you'll see when you get to the Bud Light story.

Of course, the Seuss folks weren't drinking beer because they were making champagne money off this deal. In the week after the problematic titles were pulled, Dr. Seuss accounted for six of the top ten books on Amazon's bestseller list, and thirty Seuss titles made it into the top fifty. Among them was the soon-to-be-removed *If I Ran the Zoo*, which came in at number 49, and other withdrawn books cracked the top 100, including *And to Think That I Saw It on Mulberry Street* and *Scrambled Eggs Super!*

This is why we should all pump the brakes on group outrage in any form. Oftentimes there's more nuance to the issue, and the oversimplification behind the attacks can break the compass and send everyone's efforts in the wrong direction. Think about it. A publisher pulled six of its books. Conservatives got mad at liberals for supporting the move, so they went out and made protest purchases to voice their displeasure. Ultimately it made the very company conservatives were mad at even richer than it already was.

The board members who pulled the books never said so publicly, but I don't doubt they had a good laugh about this on a boat, with a goat, on a train, and in the rain. Okay, I'll stop the Dr. Seuss puns before I get clawed to death by a Cat in a Hat.

The point is this has to be the most successful self-cancel in history, and it spawned a spin-off from the same company two years later.

Like Dr. Seuss, Roald Dahl was also one of the best-selling children's authors of all time. Books like *Charlie and the Chocolate Factory* and *James and the Giant Peach* sold over 300 million copies worldwide.

He, too, suffered an afterlife cancel of sorts when Puffin Books announced in February 2023 that Dahl's works would be rewritten to remove language deemed offensive by the publisher. According to a press release, the company hired something called "sensitivity readers" to modernize chunks of the author's text in an effort to "make sure the books can continue to be enjoyed by all today."

It's worth noting that one month before this announcement, Netflix had purchased the film rights to Dahl's book catalog for $502 million. It was hardly the price you'd pay for something that wasn't already being "enjoyed by all."

Like the self-canceling Seuss books before it, the publishers were preemptively changing their catalog to head off any potential outrage down the road. But whereas Seuss's cancellation revolved around drawings that were clearly problematic by today's standards, the brain trust behind the Dahl rewrites seemed to be inventing offenses and signaling solidarity with the word police in ways that offered no tangible improvements to any reader or character.

For instance, edits were made to any passage that described a character's physical appearance, with words like "fat" and "ugly" cut from every new edition of Dahl's books.

Augustus Gloop was no longer "enormously fat" in *Charlie and the Chocolate Factory*. From now on he was just "enormous." Either way, you're not going to be excited to sit next to him on a plane.

Mrs. Twit was originally described as "ugly and beastly" in *The Twits*, but they rewrote her description to just say "beastly." Now, I'm gonna go out on a limb and say removing the word "ugly" doesn't help anyone get a date who's still best described as "beastly." Although it might get them a set of razors and some soap.

None of this was necessary, but they didn't stop there. All gender-specific references were removed from books like *Matilda* so Miss Trunchbull, who was once described as a "most formidable female," was now just a "most formidable woman."

If you're not sure what the difference is between a female and a woman, don't feel bad, because neither is anyone who claims there *is* a difference. No, they don't usually answer that question, but they will shout you down for asking it.

What a time to be alive!

Lest all the people who menstruate have all the fun, I should mention there were also changes on the male/men side of the aisle as well:

The Oompa-Loompas in *Charlie and the Chocolate Factory*, once described as "small men," were now "small people." Again, this seemed like a misfire. If a kid reading these books has the height trajectory of an Oompa-Loompa, their gender isn't going to be the problem when they need to get something off the top shelf.

This was another cancel I got to cover all over TV. When I wasn't sucking it in every time the camera pointed at me on *America's Newsroom*, I was testifying to my experience as a parent in the modern era.

Kids don't read nearly as much as we used to, so in my opinion any classic work that gets them to put down the phone or the Xbox controller should be left alone.

America doesn't even crack the top ten in education throughout the world, despite the fact we spend more money per kid than any place on the planet. Roald Dahl's books are how millions of kids fall in love with reading, and we need all the help we can get in that department. Face it, our kids are dumber than ever, and if we're being honest, they're fatter too. The only upside is that kidnappings are down 93 percent because you can't get these pudgy bastards in the car fast enough. But there's no upside to having kids who can't read, and, incredibly, this seems to be one of the few times when the rest of the country agreed with my parenting advice.

After a week of being mocked on both sides of the political aisle for a patronizing virtue signal, Penguin Random House announced it would republish seventeen of Dahl's unedited titles as part of the Roald Dahl Classic Collection. The lone difference is that the books would now carry a disclaimer at the bottom of the copyright page that reads as follows:

> *Words matter. The wonderful words of Roald Dahl can transport you to different worlds and introduce you to the most marvelous characters. This book was written many years ago and so we regularly review the language to ensure that it can continue to be enjoyed by all today.*

Translation: Look, kids. The world is filled with a-holes who spend all day looking for something to get mad at, and we didn't want to incur their wrath. Sure, you're a kid who's just here to read a book, but we're reading the room, and it's filled with cultural arsonists. They wouldn't think twice about lighting a match to classic works that have bonded generations of people, so we had our legal team write this little preamble to signal our awareness of their existence. Anyway, we hope you enjoy a few pages of this book before you put it down to go watch TikTok videos.

Reconfiguring classic works only gives more power to the outrage mob because you're agreeing to live life on their grievance-seeking terms. But in this instance we can all take heart in knowing the publishers were wrong to think they'd have the cancel cavalry cheering them on, because in the end they were stuck with *James and the Giant Middle Finger* from both sides of the aisle.

Bravo, America.

You've still got your fastball.

Of course, no formerly acceptable work has courted more controversy than *The Dukes of Hazzard*, but, like Seuss and Dahl before it, it wasn't always that way.

When *The Dukes of Hazzard* debuted back in 1979, the show averaged 20 million viewers a week. That's a *Seinfeld*-level number in terms of viewership, and it made household names out of John Schneider, Tom Wopat, and some lady named Catherine Bach, who may or may not have had two posters hanging up in my childhood bedroom.

Some perspective on that: plenty of women have been considered gorgeous by an entire generation of Americans, but very few have been so hot, they melted a fashion staple and it was renamed in their honor.

From the second *The Dukes of Hazzard* debuted, "jean shorts" were now considered "Daisy Dukes" in every corner of the universe. It was a testament to just how good people thought she looked wearing them.

I, of course, hung the posters because of how impressed I was by her sassy, intellectual contributions, but there's no denying how many folks were drawn to her looks. Ahem.

Now, in theory, you'd expect a TV show that was famous for swashbuckling bootleggers who outran the law to be popular with a left-wing crowd that doesn't like jailing criminals. Especially when you consider how inept it portrayed the police as being.

But the Dukes did have a backward idiot of a nemesis named Jefferson Davis "Boss" Hogg. And they drove a 1969 Dodge Charger called the General Lee, nicknamed after the most popular Southern general, Robert E. Lee. It also had a Confederate flag painted on the roof, and—perhaps even more upsetting to the modern left—the car ran on gas and not electric. It also didn't have seat belts, which put them on Ralph Nader's shit list too.

Back in 1979, the General Lee wasn't viewed as an endorsement of the Confederacy so much as a depiction of a vehicle that remained popular in the South during the show's run. In fact, since *The Dukes of Hazzard* ran two years longer than the Confederacy, you could argue the symbol belongs more to the car.

Although attitudes clearly shifted on the Confederate flag over the years, reruns of the show managed to remain in syndication because people used to consider a fictitious TV show nothing more than a superficial pursuit that had zero impact in shaping society.

All of that changed in 2015 when a gun-toting lunatic killed nine people at a Black church in South Carolina. A photo found on the internet in the aftermath of the shooting showed the man draped in the Confederate flag and, as the show's narrator, Waylon Jennings, might say, "the rest was history."

Social media users began blaming the Dukes for shaping his demented worldview by displaying the flag on the General Lee. In truth, we have no idea if this madman even knew what the show was, but the second the photos surfaced, TV Land started catching all kinds of heat for continuing to carry it. Again, the horror in that church should not be minimized, but the idea that the Dukes played a role is impossible to verify. What we do know is that hundreds of millions of Americans have seen the General Lee in action and didn't run out and shoot anyone afterward.

Sadly, one lunatic zero did, and although Bo and Luke Duke were able to outrun Sheriff Rosco P. Coltrane in every single episode for seven seasons, in the end their '69 Charger was no match for the cancel crowd. The show was pulled by TV Land in June 2015 and has not appeared on broadcast television since.

It remains streamable on services like Amazon and iTunes, although there was some debate about removing it from Amazon in the aftermath of the George Floyd controversy. In the end, the streaming service decided to keep the Dukes. Many say it's because the mob was focused on modern shows like *Live PD*, but it wouldn't surprise me if Jeff Bezos was just a really big Daisy Duke fan growing up. To this day, she's probably the reason Amazon offers everyone free shipping. Bezos really wanted to send her his package. Jimmy.

Ellen

Hot damn! You're still here? I figured I'd get one or two chapters out of you, what with you spending the money and all. But to have you still on board five chapters in is a surprise nobody saw coming when HarperCollins gave a book deal to a community college graduate.

If anything, we thought that by now you'd decide the fancy cover made this a good coaster to put drinks on. Well, as Mother Teresa would say, "Butter my butt and call me a biscuit," because I'll be darned. To be clear, I'm quoting my friend's mother, Teresa. But the point is I couldn't be more appreciative. Unless of course you started reading this out of order, in which case put down the butter knife because we haven't built that kind of trust yet.

Onward!

Ellen DeGeneres built a gazillion-dollar empire with her motto of "Be kind." But backstage, the staffers reportedly lived by a motto of

"Be careful," because the Dancing Queen of Daytime was doing the Hustle when it came to her nice-gal image. Taken another way, the woman who once revealed on air that she was fifteenth cousins with Kate Middleton was even more distant from her staffers. And in the end Ellen went from cutting the rug to doing an Electric Slide in the ratings that led to the self-imposed cancellation of her show.

The problematic party started in March 2020, as it always does, on social media. Covid lockdowns were just becoming a thing, and with the country quickly running out of *Tiger King* episodes, a comedian named Kevin T. Porter attempted to fill the void. Porter tweeted a promise to make a $2 donation to the Los Angeles Regional Food Bank for every story offered up about the long-rumored tyrannical backstage behavior of Ellen, whom he described as "notoriously one of the meanest people alive."

I'm not sure if people truly believed she was awful or they just needed to take their Covid anxieties out on someone, but within a few hours the woman who'd done everything you can do in showbiz was being accused of everything you can't do backstage.

One post claimed Ellen had a sensitive nose and would send people home to shower if she didn't like the way they smelled. People were livid about this one, but I must confess I wish we had this policy at my old taxi garage.

A former teenage guest claimed a sculpture she donated to the show was later given away by Ellen as part of an on-air game. That sounds tackier than anything, but the post got a ton of traction. Then there were tales of Ellen being a monster to waitstaff, with one report claiming she once wrote a letter to a restaurant to get a girl fired for having chipped nail polish when she waited on Ellen and her wife, Portia de Rossi.

Regardless of whether or not any of this was true, people were seeing red, and even if that red needed another coat, Ellen was about to set sail on the SS *Cancel*.

Within forty-eight hours, the Twitter thread had over 2,600 complaints, and fresh off the heels of the Twitter tussle, a BuzzFeed News report cited ten former employees who claimed their old boss presided over a hostile work environment. At the time, Ellen couldn't be reached for comment because she had an intern in a headlock.

I kid, but her staffers were dead serious, claiming they were explicitly instructed to never make eye contact or speak with the host if they saw her backstage. This seemingly squared with an account by Tom Majercak, her bodyguard at the 2014 Oscars, who said Ellen was the only person he'd ever protected who didn't as much as say hi to him.

Now, in Ellen's defense, refusing to talk to your staff isn't nearly as hostile as making them watch a bunch of middle-aged white women dance during commercial breaks. No offense to Ellen's studio audience, but I've seen better moves on a U-Haul.

That being said, the perception she was out of touch with the little people grew even stronger when she posted a quarantine video that same month in which she joked that being locked down was like being in prison. Yo, Ellen, if you can't read the room, at least read the Zoom.

Because when you're broadcasting out of a $27 million mansion as the economy crumbles around you, the last thing the little people wanna hear you do is complain. I mean, as tone-deaf, woe-is-me stupidity goes, I put this at a *nine* on a scale of one to Meghan Markle.

Rumors that Ellen's show had no love for the little folks took on an even bigger life when *Everybody Loves Raymond* star Brad Garrett tweeted, *Sorry but it comes from the top. Know more than one who were treated horribly by her. Common knowledge.*

Back to the Future star Lea Thompson joined the pile on, writing, *True story.* From there, a former DJ on the show, Tony Okungbowa, scratched the record player once and for all when he posted on Instagram that he, too, had experienced all kinds of toxicity on Ellen's set.

With the entire locked-down world now trashing her on Twitter, Ellen sent an apology letter to her staff, partly to control the damage and most likely because she still didn't wanna talk to those losers face-to-face.

Warner Bros. opened up an internal investigation into the show's workplace culture in July 2020. Within weeks, three top producers were fired for their own roles in creating backstage chaos. Ellen issued a second apology to staff, this time in a video meeting in late August. With rampant speculation swirling that they might be playing taps for our favorite tap dancer, Ellen opened her new season in September 2020 with a lengthy on-air apology.

"Contrary to reports in the press and social media . . . the truth is that I am the person that you see on your TV. I am also a lot of other things. Sometimes I am sad, I get mad, I get anxious, I get frustrated, I get impatient, and I am working on all of that. I am a work in progress."

Which sounds like a fancy way of saying, *I am a complete volcano backstage that can erupt at any moment.* This would explain why all the child guests in the greenroom would play "The Floor Is Lava."

Despite her claims of compassion, Ellen's image had definitely taken a hit, and she lost nearly a million and a half viewers over the course of her eighteenth season. In May 2021, she announced that her nineteenth season would be her last.

At the time, she told the *Hollywood Reporter* she'd grown bored, saying, "When you're a creative person, you constantly need to be challenged—and as great as this show is, and as fun as it is, it's just not a challenge anymore."

There's no doubt that doing eighteen seasons of a talk show would leave anyone with a case of mission creep. But watching 1.5 million viewers fox-trot out the back door undoubtedly played a part as well.

Is Ellen really a monster? It's highly unlikely we'll ever know the truth. After all, she didn't even say what would happen to her 270 staffers. But rumor has it they applied to work someplace safer, like Ukraine.

Just a joke, Ellen.

Be kind.

Free Speech and
Farting Guards

I'm going to talk to you in this chapter about farts and cancel culture. And I know that's a strange combination, farts and cancel culture. After all, one ruins everything for everyone, and the other is farts.

Seeing as we're devoting an entire book to canceling stuff, I thought it would only be fair to offer some counterprogramming and let someone advocate for the value of censoring speech. That being said, I must confess that I didn't expect to find today's guest speaker in *Rolling Stone* magazine.

When I was a kid, *Rolling Stone* had a rebellious vibe that made every page feel like a middle finger toward the Man. The first issue I ever received in the mail was the August 1992 edition featuring a band called Body Count on the cover. They were a thrash metal group fronted by iconic rapper Ice T. They sang a wildly controversial song called "Cop Killer" that got their album pulled from a handful of stores after law enforcement organizations protested the record label's parent company, Time Warner. Seeing as I grew up in a house full of chubby but good-natured cops, I didn't agree with the band's sentiments. But reading about anti-establishment groups like Body Count and Public Enemy in *Rolling Stone* made me feel like some type of counterculture badass.

Admittedly, it didn't take much to feel like a badass in a year when the top-selling artist was Billy Ray Cyrus. He later became more famous for being Miley Cyrus's dad, but nothing his daughter ever did took a wrecking ball to pop culture half as hard as the women's prison mullet Billy Ray rocked in his "Achy Breaky Heart" video. Seriously, take off the mom jeans and save some chicks for the rest of us, bro.

If buying a copy of *Rolling Stone* in the '90s made you feel like you were raging against the Machine, doing so a few decades later feels like you are donating to the Machine.

For instance, as the Biden administration pushed a Covid vaccine mandate, the mag ran countless pieces defending Big Pharma even after the vax failed to stop transmission as advertised. They also published a pretty aggressive hit piece on Eric Clapton, who's appeared on their cover eight times, after he questioned the government's handling of the pandemic. Good luck getting through any issue without being scolded about climate change, gun control, and our white-supremacist nation.

Yes, white supremacy. Right there inside a magazine that's profiled countless minority millionaires who could only make that money because they were adored throughout the country by every walk of life, including lots and lots of white people.

RS was always a left-wing publication since its founding in San Francisco in 1967 by Jann Wenner and Ralph Gleason. But in the last ten years it has gotten so liberal, they wanted to defund the cop in the Village People. That might be a slight exaggeration on my part, but in the summer of 2020, they did publish "A Practical Guide to Defunding the Police."

You see, for a long time classic liberalism was all about defending the free expression of bands like the Clash and Black Flag and N.W.A. Nowadays, modern liberalism is more about censoring opposing viewpoints to the Democratic Party's preferred narrative of the day.

Look no further than October 2020, when the mag cheered on the censorship of Hunter Biden's laptop, calling it a "vile, baseless conspiracy theory" and chastising social media sites to do more to stop the story from spreading before the presidential election.

Never mind that the laptop turned out to be real. The anti-establishment home of sex, drugs, and rock and roll was now protecting the son of the ultimate establishment figure, who had plenty of sex and did all kinds of drugs, all because they wanted his father to rock and roll on Election Night.

While *Rolling Stone*'s preferred party did win the election, the joke was on them because Biden's not much of a rock-and-roll guy. It's hard to be when the hottest new musician the year you were born was Mozart.

If there's one thing the Biden administration loves, it's censoring speech. Not only did they push Big Tech to silence any social media accounts that questioned the efficacy of the vaccine, but they also launched a Disinformation Governance Board in the spring of 2022. It was forced to close three weeks later after it was slammed by both parties for its proposed crackdown on protected speech, but if it looks like a censorship-happy regime and it talks like a censorship-happy regime . . .

Seeing as there's been no bigger cheerleader for Joe Biden since he hit the campaign to shake invisible hands and sniff babies, we probably shouldn't be surprised that *Rolling Stone* recently published a piece explaining why cancel culture was good for society.

Again, as someone who opened their magazine to see them defending the controversial rap group 2 Live Crew and their album *Banned in the U.S.A.*, it's still a little jarring to know they're now in favor of seeing anyone who steps out of line get . . . banned in the U.S.A. But there I was in February 2023, reading a big, splashy *Rolling Stone* piece titled "Why Cancel Culture Is Good for Democracy." It was an excerpt from a book called *The Case for Cancel Culture: How This Democratic Tool Works to Liberate Us All*, written by a nice enough chap named Ernest Owens.

To be clear, I don't know the guy, but his profile picture shows him in a fine suit with a nice pocket square that went a long way with a dude like me, who just happens to be the best-dressed man in cable news. You heard me, Charles Payne.

Where were we?

Oh, yeah: Mr. Pocket Square's bullshit argument in favor of cancel culture. Owens claims cancel culture is a good thing because it "leveled the playing field for those who can't always rely on the government to protect them." Here's another news flash: the government was *never* supposed to protect anyone from anyone else's speech. The First Amendment was supposed to protect everyone's speech from the government, meaning you won't get arrested for saying things.

But he goes on to claim that, "right now, bigots are protected under the First Amendment to fuel disgusting rhetoric without state-sanctioned consequence. The America that tolerated white supremacy in their policies and laws is the same country that wants to remind us how such forms of hate are still legal via free speech. Cancel culture is the poison to those in power that have benefited from unchecked free speech."

I don't doubt that Owens's heart is in the right place, but nobody being canceled works in government. Comedians get canceled, broadcasters get canceled, musicians get canceled, sure. But the one thing they all have in common is that, like Beto O'Rourke, none of them has ever won a major election.

The only government official who's ever lost their job to what we'd call cancel culture is former comedian turned Democratic senator Al Franken. And even so, he self-canceled after a photo surfaced of him pretending to grope a sleeping woman at the height of the #MeToo movement. Now, to be clear, many of his colleagues urged him to quit, but in the end it was Franken's call alone, mainly because nobody wanted to be responsible for him returning to stand-up comedy. My word. I loved him as Stuart Smalley, but tickets to his stand-up shows are $25 to get in and $200 to get out.

As for the claim that we should be thankful for cancel culture be-cause it's a check on government behavior: Hello? We already have a check on government behavior. It's called *elections*. They are the ul-timate form of cancel culture. If you say the wrong things or do the wrong things, we can cancel you at the ballot box. But *nobody* steps down, midterm, for speech.

If you don't believe me, ask former Virginia governor Ralph Northam. In February 2019 a photo surfaced of the Democrat gov-ernor wearing a Ku Klux Klan robe in his college yearbook. Northam initially admitted it was him, only to backtrack a few days later and tell reporters he wasn't actually sure because there were two people in the photo, and one of them was wearing blackface and the other was in the Klan robe.

Oh, in that case. This is clearly a sweet prince of tolerance. A shame we even bothered him.

Get the fuck outta here!

Now, to *Rolling Stone*'s credit, the mag did trash Northam in a piece for not understanding race but in the end he finished his term without additional incident. Cancel culture doesn't ever come for the govern-ment. The problem with letting governing boards come for us and ban what they decry as hate speech is that we all have differing definitions of what it is. All too often in politics, hate speech is defined as any-thing the Democratic Party doesn't agree with.

Getting past the censorship, which is what an iconic music maga-zine is supposed to give us an outlet to do, let's take a closer look at the core argument of the piece:

"Those who fear cancel culture may claim they fear suppression of speech, but it's accountability that they want to avoid."

He's right when he says people outside the government want to avoid accountability because when it comes to free expression, there shouldn't be any accountability from the government. That's why we formed the type of government we did!

If someone writes a song that takes a position you don't like or makes a joke about a subject you don't prefer, you have every right to ignore it and move on. The idea we should be on board with firing people and destroying their careers is weapons-grade stupid and will only get dumber on the slippery slope of censorship.

Think about it. If someone is so devoid of nuance and empathy that they're willing to destroy your livelihood for *one* step out of bounds, do you really think they won't be on board with jailing you for it someday down the road?

Repeat after me:

If speech ain't free, neither are we.

On a superficial level, if we ask pop culture to conform to the rules of the progressive left, it's going to ruin everything we love in movies and music. Nobody wants to see Julia Roberts and Richard Gere star in *Pretty Person*. Nor do we wanna hear Mötley Crüe sing "Smokin' in the *Thems* Room." If you cut every offensive joke out of a movie like *Blazing Saddles*, the film would be about thirty-eight seconds long.

Allowing people to do and say anything they want not only makes for a tougher society where words don't have so much power over our lives; it gives artists the unencumbered latitude to make wildly popu-lar art that resonates with millions of people.

I didn't like the song "Fuck tha Police," but as someone who supports the cops with all the fiber in my being, I was still able to recognize that so many people *did* like the song, and I would never wanna take away their outlet.

And for all of you folks who think speech influences behavior, I can assure you, nobody Fucked the Police when my two cop brothers were single. You talk about a dry spell.

The point is, all of us—whether we're cops, cabdrivers, cable news hosts, you name it—should not be living in fear that our jobs can vanish in an instant over a joke or an unpopular opinion.

Even if you're truly talking out of your ass, like a Florida man named Doug who was fired from his hospital security job for recording his farts and posting them on Instagram.

Yes, I know this subject matter seems a little highbrow, given the intellect of this book so far, but if we're gonna talk about free expression, it's only fair that we zero in on a guy who truly let it rip in life. Back in 2018, the thirty-one-year-old Florida man began recording dozens of farts a day and sending them to a group chat to entertain his friends. If you're wondering where he got the firepower to fart as often as he did, you've never eaten hospital food.

As for Doug, he ate enough to have a physique that resembled the Kevin James character in the movie *Paul Blart: Mall Cop*, which earned him the nickname "Paul Flart" from the recipients of his Wind-stagrams.

But what started out as a goofy gimmick he shared with next to no followers quickly exploded, in more ways than one, after someone shared his video to a popular Reddit page.

From there he made a mad dash to 100,000 followers and presumably the bathroom.

You might wonder why the world latched onto this fragrant phenom as passionately as it did. The truth is, to a lot of people, farts are inherently funny. Sure, most of those people are two years old, but there's clearly an older audience because Paul's Flarts had millions of views in a matter of days.

Unfortunately, one of those newfound sets of eyeballs belonged to his employer. Let's just say his boss was not a fan, even if he felt like turning one on.

In August 2018, less than two months after he became an internet sensation, our hero was posting an Instagram Live video when his supervisor interrupted it to fire him right there at his desk after watching him post the content in their workspace.

I'm sure their sense of sight wasn't as much of a driving force as their sense of smell, but the point is Paul Flart the employee was no more.

Yes, the account still exists on Instagram and boasts 99,000 followers to this day. Sure, I could make a zillion puns to keep this chapter going, but the point is the point:

Nobody is better off in a world where not even a gassy guard can get cancel culture to turn the other cheek.

Good night, everybody.

Gilbert, Griffin, and Gillis

Depending on who you ask, Gilbert Gottfried was either a creative genius who mined the most depraved topics for comedy gold or a crazed man-child stuck in a perpetual state of arrested development. People who knew him best would tell you the correct answer was both.

I had the honor of opening for Gilbert a few times at Carolines on Broadway in Times Square. I'm happy to say our shows went so well that Carolines is now a racquetball club. True story, although they went out of business over a decade later, so don't look at us.

Gilbert was what's known as a "comic's comic." It's a nice way of saying he liked to tell jokes that were *way* too dark for an audience of civilians but would crush with the guys in the greenroom. By the way, if you're wondering why so many comics enjoy joking about sad subject matters, you've never seen their childhoods. I'll spare you the grim details, but it's safe to say that comedians are to good childhoods what the Kennedys are to good driving. That was a Ted Kennedy joke, for those of you under fifty. He was JFK's younger brother, and a forty-six-year senator who made quite a splash in politics. But we're here to talk Gilbert, so as Ted Kennedy's passengers might say, we need to get this show back on the road.

There's a legendary story where Gilbert once horrified a crowd by telling jokes about the masturbation arrest of the late great Paul Reubens, aka Pee-wee Herman. The good news is, as always, they killed backstage. The bad news is it happened during a live broadcast of the 1991 Emmy Awards. Producers were forced to issue an apology, and that same night he was told he'd never be invited back.

Rolling Stone reported that Gilbert was blacklisted from awards shows because of what he did in the theater. Although, in his defense, it's still a lot better than what Paul got caught doing in the theater.

Like all great comics, Gilbert didn't live by the motto "Read the room"; he always saw comedy as an opportunity to "lead the room." Although sometimes he took it in the wrong direction by design.

At the Friars Club roast of Hugh Hefner, which took place just a few weeks after the terror attacks of September 11, 2001, Gilbert joked that he couldn't get a direct flight because "they said they have to stop at the Empire State Building first." If you find yourself cringing or yelling, "Too soon," you can multiply that revulsion by 100 and you still won't have a sense of how the audience felt in October 2001.

Sensing their disgust, he ditched his prepared remarks and launched into a famously filthy street joke called "The Aristocrats." If you're not familiar, it's an old showbiz tale designed to horrify listeners by subjecting them to an endless litany of smutty sex acts.

Gilbert's telling of the joke that night included phrases I wouldn't repeat to you if we were celebrating our twentieth anniversary as prison bunkmates. It's that far out there. Let's just say that at one point women are doing things with dogs that they don't do with their husbands. And if they do, I married the wrong woman.

Incredibly, the smuttier he got, the sillier the whole thing became, and by the end of it, he'd won the entire room back. I mean, he absolutely crushed.

The Aristocrats routine went over so well, it inspired a documentary about the history of the joke that was released in theaters and featured some of the funniest comics who ever lived, as well as Whoopi Goldberg.

You see, for all of Gilbert's talents, his one true superpower was never backing down. Nobody on earth gave less of a fuck than he did when it came to offending people, mainly because he knew that, in the end, the only thing he was really guilty of was trying to entertain. He knew that comedy wasn't about boundaries; it was about bedlam, and the whole point was not to care.

Onstage, Gilbert truly didn't, in any way—which is why he was the only guy who could open his set with a September 11 joke that repulsed the world and close with a standing ovation.

Despite his penchant for flying too close to the sun—on a hijacked plane no less—Gilbert did manage to have dozens of major mainstream successes in his career. He stole the show from Eddie Murphy in the summer blockbuster *Beverly Hills Cop II* and went on to appear in countless box office smashes, including Disney's *Aladdin*.

He made over one hundred appearances on *The Howard Stern Show* back when it was a really big deal. To give you some perspective, Stern was so huge in his terrestrial radio days, he referred to himself as the "King of All Media," and nobody could argue. Since moving to Sirius XM, he's become such a grievance-oriented diva that he's more like the "Prince Harry of All Media," but audiences loved Gilbert no matter which Howard he had to deal with.

Like few comics before him but thousands after, Gilbert's problems didn't start until he joined Twitter and began commenting on topics that not everyone could "like."

In March 2011, Gilbert was voicing the Aflac duck in a series of commercials for the insurance company when the largest recorded earthquake in the history of Japan occurred, triggering a tsunami that reached heights of 133 feet and killing over 19,000 people. The tsunami also caused the meltdown of the Fukushima nuclear power plant and forced the evacuation of hundreds of thousands of residents.

I know what you're thinking.

Who's ready for some comedy?

Okay, so you might not have been thinking that, but Gilbert definitely was, so he took to Twitter and started rattling off jokes. This is what comics do. We use laughter as a coping mechanism to take power away from horrific events we don't have the desire or the emotional capacity to process straight up.

I completely understand that not everybody rolls this way, and they have every right to ignore this sort of content. What I'll never understand is wanting to take this coping mechanism away from the people who do laugh at tragedies because we all gotta get by somehow.

Unfortunately for Gilbert, I didn't work on the board of directors at Aflac, which just so happened to do 75 percent of its business in Japan at the time of the disaster.

I seriously doubt the Japanese people were concerned with jokes being told on the other side of the world, as their side was literally underwater. But it still wasn't a good look for the company to have its spokesperson tweeting things in the aftermath of a tsunami like:

Japan is really advanced. They don't go to the beach; the beach comes to them.

My girlfriend broke up with me. But like they say in Japan, another one will come floating by any minute now.

Did he go too far? Definitely. That was his entire ethos onstage. The problem with social media is comics are now telling jokes outside the comedy club's circle of trust. Not everybody in the digital audience has bought two drinks and agreed that none of this should be taken seriously.

Aflac hadn't shaken hands on that deal, either, so he was fired immediately. To quote Gilbert, "My agent called and said my tsunami jokes were doing great in America but over in Japan they were sinking."

Nobody cared less than him.

Gilbert Gottfried may be the first major celebrity who lost a gig because of Twitter, but he wasn't anywhere near the last.

Like Gilbert, Kathy Griffin also had a major run in showbiz, and you could almost argue that hers was more impressive because she did it with a lot less talent. Don't get me wrong, she was always funny in clubs and witty enough to host a self-aware hit show called *My Life on the D-List*. Heck, she even had a job co-hosting New Year's Eve on the biggest comedy channel in the world: CNN.

Kathy, like just about everyone else in Hollywood, was a raging liberal who couldn't make peace with the election of Donald Trump. They thought the presidency was Hillary Clinton's birthright, and it seemed unfathomable that in a time when anyone could be canceled for tweeting anything even mildly offensive, we had somehow elected a guy to the highest office in the land who might have had the most offensive account in the history of Twitter.

Earlier in the book we mentioned the old saying "Defense wins championships." Judging from his posts, Trump has never heard it. This guy went on the offense against everything, from the legitimacy of Barack Obama's birth certificate to the appearance of just about every woman who criticized him. At the very first debate of the Republican primary season he was asked by Fox moderator Megyn Kelly how he could expect women to vote for him seeing as he'd referred to them in the past as dogs and pigs and slobs, to which he replied, "Only Rosie O'Donnell."

It brought down the house and just about any chance his opponents had of stopping him.

Trump's election was at least in some way a reaction to the rampant speech policing that engulfed our nation in the infancy of social media. The years leading up to his nomination saw so many people lose their jobs for tweeting things that his willingness to give a giant middle finger to "the haters and the losers" made him the ultimate punk rock candidate to so many people.

Nobody could defend everything Trump tweeted, but by then they were tired of having to defend anything *anyone* tweeted. As hard as it is to imagine now, there was a time when none of us had to keep a law firm on retainer in our heads twenty-four hours a day to pore over every word that came out of our mouths for fear it could get us in trouble. Prior to social media, words were just words, and people were just happier.

Trump was a throwback to that era, and he represented the ultimate irony for the cancel crowd. They'd overzealously targeted the rank and file so hard that when an actual presidential candidate came along who really did take it too far on more than one (hundred) occasions, they were powerless to stop him. The more Trump tweeted, the more the media freaked out, the more his appeal grew with regular folks who were tired of the moral indignation from a leadership class that sold them into countless wars while selling out their jobs along the way.

Having said that, hardly anybody expected Trump to win, including Trump. When our nation woke up the morning after the election to see Hillary conceding in her purple suit, we were all a little thrown off. Nobody looked more out of sorts than Bill Clinton, who was so excited to get his new office set up that he'd already begun measuring the interns.

In the days and weeks after Trump's win, the celebrity activist crowd Kathy Griffin belonged to seemingly started a contest to see who could freak out the most in public. We all know about the pussy hats women wore to signal their oppression under Trump. But the truth is, men wore pussy hats too. Although, judging by the looks of these guys, I'm pretty sure they didn't know what the thing on their head was. Let's just say that the last time these fellas saw a bush, it had a vice president named Cheney.

Nobody took the era of hats and hysteria further than Griffin, who posted an image on Twitter that showed her holding what appeared to be Trump's severed head. To be clear, the whole thing was completely plastic. But as for *Trump's face*, this was a grotesque image. So much so that news networks didn't even show it on TV, choosing instead to blur it out as a means of shielding people from the disgustingness of it all. The image may have been fake, but the backlash was real, with tens of thousands of people on both sides of the aisle trashing the comic for crossing a line. Trump even dove in headfirst, some pun intended, tweeting:

> *Kathy Griffin should be ashamed of herself. My children, especially my 11 year old son Barron, are having a hard time with this. Sick!*

The blowback was big enough that Griffin posted a video apology saying, "I sincerely apologize. I am just now seeing the reaction to these images. I'm a comic. I crossed the line. I moved the line, then I crossed it. I went way too far."

Despite the "woe-is-me-a culpa," her comedy tour was canceled and she lost her endorsement deal with Squatty Potty, which had to leave her down in the dumps. I'll show myself out.

CNN fired her from her long-running gig co-hosting New Year's Eve with Anderson Cooper. And to top it all off, the woman who hosted a show called *My Life on the D-List* was temporarily put on the government's no-fly list.

History will record it as the first and only time that anyone was con-

victed in the court of public opinion for targeting Donald Trump—
and, let's face it, you never forget your first. Unless it was with Bill
Cosby.

Oh, come on, Jimmy!

Shane Gillis *might* laugh at that absurd joke. He's a delightfully
dark comic who is one of the rare acts who's loved by comedians
and audiences. This dude is super talented, which makes it shocking
that he wound up getting hired by *Saturday Night Live* in the first
place.

Don't get me wrong: *SNL* has churned out some of the biggest
comedy stars in the history of the world, but in the past ten years it's
been as funny as an orphanage on fire on Christmas Day.

There was hope in the stand-up community that *SNL* could be getting its groove back when they hired Gillis in the fall of 2019 to star
in the show's forty-fifth season. He didn't come from the liberal grievance rooms of the alternative comedy scene. Nor was he discovered in
mediums outside of comedy, like Improv.

Once again, things were looking up, until people started looking around the internet. Less than one week after his hiring was announced, someone dug up a series of old podcast recordings in which
he used slurs for Asian people and uttered some homophobic phrases
to describe his fellow comics.

Are these terms I'd admit to using in jokes over the years?

Not in a printed book. Are you crazy?

But to be clear, he didn't attack anyone. He didn't issue a call to action; he told dumb jokes. For my money, the bigger threat to society is
the class of people who get out of bed looking to destroy anyone who
achieves something in showbiz that they themselves couldn't dream
of pulling off.

They're the only ones looking to harm someone's well-being, and
they pulled it off in Shane Gillis's case. A few days after he was named
to the cast of its forty-fifth season, *SNL* announced that Gillis was the

first person in history to be fired from the show before ever appearing in a sketch.

To his credit, he owned the dubious honor, tweeting:

I'm a comedian who was funny enough for SNL. That can't be taken away. Of course I wanted an opportunity to prove myself at SNL, but I understand it would be too much of a distraction. I respect the decision they made. I'm honestly grateful for the opportunity. I was always a Mad TV guy anyway.

The truth is we've *all* said off-color things, whether we want to admit it or not. And while he clearly used words that have always been offensive, it still seems excessive that a guy who worked his ass off to achieve the Holy Grail of comedy was denied a seat at the table simply because someone dug up a series of crass jokes he made in the infancy stages of his development. Again, you've gotta look at comics like they're chefs because jokes are absolutely like recipes. Sometimes the ingredients don't add up to a killer meal, but it's not because the chef is trying to kill the customers. Although I do have my doubts about the guys at White Castle.

But seriously, why not suspend Shane? Maybe even work it into a sketch in which they mock him for needing to learn? If anything, it would raise more awareness and maybe even give direction to a future generation of comics.

That would be a happy compromise, but the truth is the cancel crowd doesn't want compromise or even a step in the right direction. They want power, not progress.

Think about it. Gillis was canceled because someone dug up old jokes about Asians and gays. Yet none of the people doing that digging or getting offended organized any type of outreach to the Asian community. Nor did they do anything whatsoever for the gay community. *Zero.* Not even a champagne brunch, a karaoke party, or a *Golden Girls* marathon.

Now, you could argue that Gillis's firing was a sign of progress if, say, they replaced him with a gay or Asian cast member, but *SNL* didn't replace him at all.

And nobody said a word because, in the end, the outrage mob isn't here to protect people or improve things. They're here to gain relevance by pretending to care more than you do. They pull it off by overreacting to borderline things. They treat jokes as hate crimes—not because they think they are, but because they think it's effective.

Which is why nothing has gotten better for any marginalized group the cancel crowd has sprung into action on behalf of. In fact, it's rare that anyone facing real adversity would even latch onto a cancel effort.

Why?

Because if your community is *truly* suffering, the last thing you have time to do is look at what people are tweeting while they're killing time on the toilet.

I promise you, no one going through a tsunami had time to care that Gilbert Gottfried was joking about getting dumped on the other side of the world, saying something along the lines of *Breakups are easier during a tsunami, because you know there's other fish in the sea. And the living room. And the garage.*

These sorts of throwaway lines only become completely unforgivable because the cancel crowd denies people perspective. They overwhelm us with angry tweets and make everyone a prisoner of the moment, unable to see that the current rage cycle won't last forever. It's this collective psychology of doom that causes corporations to fire people because they just want the bad PR to go away. Of course, the cancels are always sold to us in the aftermath as a protective gesture, and that part *is* true: The executives are covering their asses.

Sadly for us normal people who understand the difference between a joke and a hate crime, the mob rule mentality is not only claiming the jobs of people like Gilbert and Gillis; it's taking away everyone else's sense of humor. And while I've never loved Kathy Griffin's politics, I absolutely hate that her terrible joke gave the outrage mob a head start.

Houston Rockets

The NBA has been no stranger to political activism over the years. However, many fans wish professional basketball players would stick to doing what they do best: the Kardashians.

Nothing against Kim, Khloé, and their Instagram gang. But when it comes to fighting injustices, the NBA has been throwing a no-look pass on the biggest human rights abuses in the world, all so they can cash out in Communist China.

Nobody knows this better than former Houston Rockets general manager Daryl Morey, who inadvertently got all of his team's games canceled by the Chinese government in 2019.

I'll explain the story in a second, but let me just say that as a New York Knicks fan, I've definitely wished the government did us all a favor and pulled their games off TV from time to time. You know you root for a bad team when their biggest advertiser is a suicide prevention hotline.

The Rockets did get benched by a government, but they definitely weren't looking out for their fans when it happened. No, the franchise was incredibly popular in China, dating back to 2002, when the team drafted superstar center Yao Ming with the first pick of the NBA draft. At seven feet six inches tall, Ming had been a huge sensation on the Chinese national team. When he joined the NBA, his jersey became an instant bestseller around the country. The Rockets became so popular during his career that, even after he retired, the team remained a top TV attraction in China.

All of that changed in October 2019 when pro-democracy protesters took to the streets of Hong Kong to mark the seventieth anniversary of the People's Republic of China. Or, as Donald Trump calls it, *Chai*-nuh.

Cracks me up every time. At issue was a new law that would allow criminal offenders in Hong Kong to be extradited to mainland China. Now, some of you might ask, *Yo, Jimmy, I thought Hong Kong was in China?*

Depends on who you ask! The Chinese government has a "one country, two systems" policy that's supposed to allow Hong Kong to have its own economic and criminal justice systems that are independent from that of the Chinese Communist Party. The deal was made between China and the United Kingdom when control of Hong Kong was decided in the 1980s.

Thanks, Google!

Fast-forward back to 2019, and many Hong Kong residents feared that shipping criminals into China's jurisdiction could become a problem, given the Communist Party's history of suppressing political dissent. What's to stop China from jailing Hong Kong's citizens for the heck of it, as they're kind of sort of known to do? And what does all of this have to do with the NBA? you ask.

Slow your roll, pal, I'm getting there. You're asking so many questions, I'm starting to think *you're* writing a book. Seriously, WTF?

Here's the deal: the protests started sporadically the previous spring, but by the fall of 2019 they had morphed into the single largest demonstration in the nation's history. Some estimates claimed there were over a million people in the streets. Picture San Francisco if everyone hanging out on the sidewalks went to the bathroom *indoors*.

The peaceful demonstrations eventually turned violent when activists clashed with military troops that had been sent in to "calm things down." When communist governments send troops to a protest, it's a polite way of saying, "Wrap things up before we wrap it up for you."

The protesters weren't ready to go home, so as the sidewalk skirmishes increased, international observers became concerned that we could be headed toward a sequel to the Tiananmen Square massacre of 1989, where thousands of student protesters were killed by the Chinese army.

Back in America, thousands of people tweeted their support for the protesters (and then immediately got to work trying to figure out what they were actually protesting). Many even put Hong Kong's flag in their bio in an effort to score "likes" from other people like themselves who couldn't find Hong Kong on a map of Hong Kong. Of course, there were plenty of folks genuinely invested in the cause, and one of them just so happened to be the general manager of the most popular NBA team in mainland China, aka the Houston Rockets.

On Friday, October 4, 2019, with millions of people flooding the streets and thousands of them being jailed for doing so, Daryl Morey tweeted: *Fight for Freedom. Stand with Hong Kong.*

It sounds like an innocent enough take, but that's because you don't live in a communist country, try as AOC might. China's Twitter referees called a personal foul on Morey, and just like that, what started out as a throwaway tweet in the middle of a slow Friday news cycle quickly spiraled into a full-on international incident.

You see, communist governments take criticism about as well as a cat takes a bath, meaning they want whoever's responsible for it killed.

Someone must have told Morey this because he deleted the tweet and issued an apology a few hours later. By then the cat's ears were flat and its claws were all the way out. Not good. Within twenty-four hours, the CCP had pulled all Rockets games from TV and several companies, including the country's biggest retailer, Alibaba, also severed ties with the NBA, undoubtedly done at the behest of the Communist Party.

This was a huge problem for the league because the NBA is believed to make $5 billion a year in China. It might be even higher, judging by how quickly league spokesperson Mike Bass fired off an apology statement that read as follows:

"We recognize that the views expressed by Houston Rockets General Manager Daryl Morey have deeply offended many of our friends and fans in China, which is regrettable. While Daryl has made it clear that his Tweet does not represent the Rockets or the NBA, the values of the league support individuals' educating themselves and sharing their views on matters important to them. We have great respect for the history and culture of China and hope that sports and the NBA can be used as a unifying force to bridge cultural divides and bring people together."

Translation: I know our league has a social justice coalition with a stated goal of raising awareness of injustice around the world, but *please*, communist government that's considered the biggest human rights abusers on the planet, don't pull the plug on us because we're nothing without your TV money. After all, your fondness for slave labor makes most of our sneakers in the factories. We need each other!

I wish I was kidding, but if you ever want to feel truly let down by the human race—like, worse than you do after watching *The View*—read a few paragraphs from the United Nations Human Rights Council's report on China's treatment of Uyghur Muslims. It was published in 2022 and found that China's actions toward the minority group constituted *crimes against humanity*. This report is not a secret to anyone at the woke corporations doing business in Beijing, but—rather than ruining your week with horrific details—let's just say history will show that when the game of human rights was on the line, the NBA shot an airball.

Lawmakers from both political parties said so in a rare display of bipartisanship. Florida senator Marco Rubio tweeted that the NBA was throwing Morey under the bus to appease the Communist Chinese government and called it "grotesque." He was joined by Missouri senator Josh Hawley, Texas senator Ted Cruz, and Florida senator Rick Scott.

Heck, Democratic senator Chuck Schumer took time out from his busy schedule of looking like a villain on *The Simpsons* to tweet: *No one should implement a gag rule on Americans speaking out about freedom.* Democratic senator Ron Wyden of Oregon also slammed the league. Even Massachusetts senator Elizabeth Warren bashed the NBA for cutting Morey off. And let's face it, if anyone knows about getting cut off, it's someone who drives in Boston. Let's just say they call those drivers "Mass-holes" for a reason.

All of the China criticisms seemed to fly over the head of LeBron James, who leads the league every year in virtue signaling but who immediately called for a technical on Daryl Morey for supporting pro-democracy protesters.

Prior to his team's game that Sunday, King James told reporters: "We talk about this freedom of speech. Yes, we all do have freedom of speech. But at times, there are ramifications for the negative that can happen when you're not thinking about others, and you're only thinking about yourself.

"I don't want to get into a word or sentence feud with Daryl Morey. But I believe he wasn't educated on the situation at hand, and he spoke . . ."

Every once in a while, LeBron finds a creative way to remind us that he's so good at basketball he was able to skip college. This was one of those moments. Nothing says *I've never spent time in a classroom* like claiming Morey was thinking about himself when he expressed support for protesters who were literally risking their lives to stand up to a truly oppressive government.

Unlike America, where guys like LeBron and Colin Kaepernick trash our cops and get rewarded with sneaker deals, government protesters in China get rewarded with hard labor camps at best and firing squads at worst.

When it comes to protesting in China, Nike's motto is not "Just Do It." No, they save that line for the "affordable laborers" sewing their sneakers in the factory: *I don't care if you're tired and underpaid: "Just Do It!"*

If anyone wasn't "educated on the situation" in China, it was LeBron. Either that, or he just looked the other way like the rest of the league executives who decided there's no point in being social justice warriors if a country stops selling jerseys from the Golden State Warriors.

This is the problem with corporate activism as a whole: oftentimes when they take positions on domestic issues in this country, they're engaging in a championship level of hypocrisy, given their willingness to do business in other places where the problems are infinitely worse.

For instance, Disney went to war with Florida governor Ron DeSantis for passing a "Parental Rights in Education" bill that banned instruction on sexuality of any kind for children from kindergarten to third grade. Democrats dubbed it the "Don't Say Gay" bill and claimed DeSantis was outlawing gayness.

First of all, anybody who believes Florida has banned gay people has never been to Key West. Second, the idea of Disney attacking anyone for their take on gay rights is richer than the custard they sell you for $12 a cone on Main Street. Their Disney+ streaming service does business in twelve countries that criminalize gay activity and, in some instances, punish it with chemical castration or even death.

Folks, if two guys begin their day holding hands in Yemen, they do not close it with a happy ending. Well, they might, but they better hope the cops don't catch them in the act.

The point is corporations like Disney and the NBA love to chase social justice points, but their race to the cash register in places where people's rights are truly under assault is why nobody should ever take them seriously.

Houston Rockets games did ultimately return to the airwaves in China fifteen months and a dozen groveling apologies from the NBA later. In that time Daryl Morey left the Houston Rockets to work with the Philadelphia 76ers—and not in their social media department.

In an ongoing effort to demonstrate its commitment to the betterment of humanity, the NBA has since approved a dozen social justice slogans for players to wear on the backs of their jerseys during games.

On any given night, you can sit in the stands, drinking a $25 beer while a guy who makes $40 million to play a children's game runs by you in a jersey that lectures *you* about "injustice." Bring a life preserver, because you might drown in the irony. If you do survive, you can then see a guy named "Freedom" pass the ball to a guy named "Power to the People."

Provided those freedom-loving, power-seeking people aren't in Hong Kong, of course. You see, just like its players, the NBA's social justice values never get called for "traveling."

Influencers

Merriam-Webster defines an influencer as "a person who inspires or guides the actions of others." A good example would be Kim Kardashian, who's so famous she earns $1.5 million to endorse a product in a single Instagram post. Sure, people like to mock Kim for rising to fame off a sex tape, but I've got nothing but respect for her because this is a woman who truly started from the bottom. In more ways than one.

If we could get serious for a second, the term "influencer" rose to prominence thanks to social media, which spawned an entirely different type of celebrity spokesperson.

You see, before there was Instagram, Facebook, and Twitter, Americans had this thing called privacy. We lived our lives in relative anonymity, and it was patently *unthinkable* to imagine sharing your dog's birthday or your kid's art project with thousands of strangers you'd never met. Then social media came along and inspired us all to start our own personal news networks that broadcast every detail of our lives with no regard for the fact that none of it really needs to be shared. Strange as it may seem now, there was a time when you knew the world would be okay if you didn't hand them an unsolicited list of your top five Aerosmith songs.

Unfortunately, anybody who thinks we're going back to that time can Dream On because Facebook put us on a never-ending hamster wheel of oversharing. Questions, comments, conspiracy theories—all of it shared in pursuit of the digital dopamine we call "likes."

Prior to social media, all we had was "happiness."

Now the whole world is cranky from working full-time paparazzi jobs in which we follow *ourselves* around in search of breaking news our followers might enjoy. First, there was TMZ. Now there's ME-M-Z.

We no longer keep up with the Kardashians. We *are* the Kardashians.

What I always found funny is that most of the behavior that gets rewarded on these apps would get you put into a home before social media became a thing. Take the people who post dinner pictures all the time:

Twenty-five years ago, if you were to take a picture of your dinner, go and get it *developed*, and then drive back to a group of people, they'd be, like, *What the hell is wrong with you?* Now you post that pasta and never question how insane you look.

TikTok is another example. If you would've shared a video of yourself dancing with your cat ten years ago, they wouldn't click *subscribe* on your profile; they'd click *handcuffs* on your wrists and cart you and the cat off to a nuthouse.

Social media completely upended our definition of acceptable behavior and made relevance way more important than competence. Your local restaurant could suck, but it still has a line around the building because the chef is some hot foreign guy whose ponytail went viral on Instagram.

Anyone can become a celebrity for doing anything these days—even going to prison with a violent arrest record. Just ask Jeremy Meeks, a member of the Crips street gang who became a fashion model after his mug shot went viral.

Meeks was arrested on felony weapons charges in 2014, but when the Stockton, California, police department posted his sexy-ass mug shot online, the photo garnered 95,000 likes in twenty-four hours. It was the most in the history of the site, which prompted BuzzFeed News to do a story about the dreamy delinquent, at which point Twitter responded with the trending hashtag #FelonCrushFridays.

Just like that, twenty-four hours after his latest arrest, career criminal Jeremy Meeks had become the viral sensation known as the "Hot Felon." Major modeling agencies began calling him on a day when he'd normally be calling his lawyer.

What a time to be alive!

The Hot Felon served just under two years for a felony weapons conviction, which went on his record right next to a prior charge for assaulting a minor. Never mind all that because the internet had spoken.

When he finished the sentence, he walked out of prison and onto the fashion runways of New York, Milan, and Paris while the rest of his peers were modeling orange jumpsuits on the side of a highway.

He also became one of the most sought-after bachelors on the planet, although you should be careful, ladies, because this guy will steal your heart. (And your car.)

Social media has turned life into a lottery drawing for anybody who buys a ticket. And while most users have spent the past decade pretending they were celebrities, some people actually pulled it off in major ways. These are the folks who inspired the term "influencer." Their content is so popular that companies pay them millions of dollars to share one post with their massive followings.

Some of them were already famous outside of social media, like Portuguese soccer star/super hunk Cristiano Ronaldo. He's considered the highest-paid influencer in the world, bringing in an average of $3.92 million for a single post to his 545 million followers. It's crazy to think you can get 545 million followers for running around a soccer field, yet Jesus walked on water, and he had only twelve followers. That's my time, be sure to try the veal here at the last supper!

Kylie Jenner has the top spot here in America and is said to be pulling down $1.8 million for a single post to her 379 million followers. She's endorsed Puma, PacSun, and Calvin Klein, and when she launched her own line of Kylie Cosmetics, she became the world's youngest billionaire. In fact to this day, the only person who's accomplished more is George Santos. Although he was dealing with a different kind of "makeup."

But even people from less traditional backgrounds than sports and Hollywood have cultivated massive followings thanks to nothing more than their social media reach. Khaby Lame is a Senegalese-Italian influencer who rose to fame during Covid lockdowns for mocking the "life hack" videos people post on TikTok. He's currently the most followed account in the history of TikTok with over 142 million followers, and he earns $400,000 for a single post on behalf of companies like Xbox, Netflix, and Amazon. The girl he passed for the top spot on TikTok, Charli D'Amelio, was a competitive dancer who exploded in popularity after she began posting lip-syncing videos. D'Amelio has landed endorsement deals with Valentino, Prada, and Burberry, and also launched her own clothing brand called Social Tourist. She's not yet old enough to buy a beer, but she could definitely buy the bar, and the one across the street.

The point is, people are making absolutely mad money on social media, but unfortunately these influencer-inspired campaigns don't always have the positive impact on sales that brands are hoping for.

If you don't believe me, you're one of the few people still drinking Bud Light.

Talk about a backfire.

For decades, Budweiser marketed itself as the "King of Beers," although its offshoot, Bud Light, consistently outsold it. Bud Light pulled in $4.8 billion in 2022 alone, while Budweiser went home with $1.83 billion. To be fair, that's still better than a lot of the things I've gone home with after a night of Budweiser.

Don't judge me. It's a long season. Nobody goes undefeated.

Of course, these sales numbers came in before Bud Light's marketing team green-lit a beer can with an image of transgender TikTok influencer Dylan Mulvaney on the side. Fans of history will note that this was the moment when social media went full French Revolution on the King of Beers, sending any and all profits to the guillotine.

For a bit of background, Dylan Mulvaney was a showbiz prospector no different than myself and some of the misfit toys I call friends. As a male actor, Mulvaney attended all kinds of casting calls and made some solid inroads by being cast in *The Book of Mormon* and competing on *The Price Is Right*.

Which is to say that while Dylan Mulvaney the man was getting work, nobody had heard of the guy. All of that changed when he announced he'd become a gal. To be clear, I'm not saying Mulvaney transitioned for strategic purposes, but it did turn out to be an absolutely brilliant business strategy. When Mulvaney began documenting the process on TikTok, the account exploded to 10 million followers and a series of major endorsements quickly followed.

Nike had Mulvaney endorsing women's yoga pants, which seemed like a bit of a stretch, some pun intended. Tampax tampons sent over a few endorsement bucks, which also seemed a little off to anyone who's ever passed a biology class.

Then Bud Light came along and told these scientifically challenged marketing campaigns to hold my beer. The rest is history, including the head of Bud Light's marketing team.

The can in question was announced on Mulvaney's TikTok account in March 2023. The influencer posted a video during the NCAA March Madness basketball tournament, telling viewers that Bud Light sent the gift to commemorate "one year of girlhood."

So technically speaking, Bud Light was giving beer to a one-year-old girl. I'm not sure that's what alcohol commercials mean by "drink responsibly," but the company would later claim the can was supposed to show how "beer brings people together." The good news for Bud is they were right about their ability to unite just about everyone who drank their beer. The bad news is a prolonged boycott that stayed together for a lot longer than most of the couples who were united by beer the old-fashioned way.

Now, if you've seen the famous clip of Mulvaney on *The Price Is Right*, you'll understand why Bud Light had to have known it would turn political when they basically said, *This is the one person in America worthy of putting on a Bud Light can.* Mulvaney was the poster person for the left's identity politics movement. It'd be one thing if they'd chosen to highlight some right-wing figures to level things out, but even that would've been a huge misfire.

The best explanation of why comes from Fox Business host and beer enthusiast Brian Brenberg, who was a guest on *Gutfeld!* while yours truly was guest hosting for Greg:

"Beer is not for activists. It's for *in-activists*."

Let the record show that Fox Business hosts are better at reading markets than actual marketing executives by a wide margin. Within hours of the can's debut on TikTok, Bud Light was getting shotgunned, and not the way you do before a concert or a *really* important business meeting.

Just me on that one?

Kid Rock posted a video that quickly went viral in which he and friends shot up several cases of Bud Light. Other musicians like country legend Travis Tritt followed suit in declaring he wouldn't be drinking it "Anymore." (That's a Travis Tritt song for the non–country fans in the audience.) Along the way, an amazing radio show called *Fox Across America with Jimmy Failla* tacked on a brilliant parody of Bud Light's "Real Men of Genius" that made its own big splash across the country.

Point being, if Bud was the King of Beers, Bud Light was now the Rodney King of Beers.

Dammit, Jimmy.

Things only got worse when a podcast surfaced of the company's new vice president of marketing, Alissa Heinerscheid, explaining that she chose Mulvaney as a means of "freshening up the brand."

Speaking to the *Make Yourself at Home* podcast on March 30, Heinerscheid explained the change, saying: "We had this hangover. I mean, Bud Light had been kind of a brand of fratty, kind of out-of-touch humor, and it was really important that we had another approach."

Because nothing wins back furious customers like calling them fratty and out of touch! Like, I've never read a crisis management book, but something tells me there's not a passage that encourages companies to court fleeing customers by yelling, *Wait, you guys suck! Come back!*

I should also point out to Ms. Heinerscheid that we have different definitions of a branding "hangover." Bud Light was the top-selling domestic beer in the country when she gave this campaign the go-ahead. Fast-forward a month, and sales had dropped by 29 percent, and she'd taken billions of dollars off the market cap of its parent company, Tranheuser-Busch.

The company issued several apologies and aired a patronizing commercial that appealed to the perceived patriotism of its customers. The ad featured a Clydesdale running through wheat fields, the Gateway Arch, even the World Trade Center in New York City. America definitely loves its horses, but in this case it didn't like the idea that *Mister* Ed might drink a can of Bud Light and begin identifying as *Missus* Ed.

I kid, but Bud Light was not playing when they put both Alissa Heinerscheid and her boss, Daniel Blake, vice president of marketing for Bud, on administrative leave. The *Wall Street Journal* reported that the leave was not voluntary, meaning this was the company's call.

That being said, Bud's top executives did try to claim it was *not* their call to put Mulvaney on a commemorative beer can, saying the decision was made by a third-party marketing firm without their knowledge. I'm not sure why they decided to go with such an absurd defense, but my sources tell me they flipped a coin between that and blaming it all on Spuds Mackenzie. (That one was for everyone who grew up in the '80s.)

The real problem is that companies are hiring woke marketing executives who have a different set of priorities than their actual customers. Whereas Bud Light drinkers just wanted a cold one at the beginning of a ball game or the end of a long shift, these marketing executives want commercials that push the social justice initiative known as DEI.

DEI is supposed to stand for "Diversity, Equity, and Inclusion," but in Bud Light's case it stands for "Don't Encourage Influencers"— because, in doing so, the number one domestic beer stepped in number two.

Bud Light's defenders tried to characterize the backlash as some sort of transphobia but, please. Customers weren't mad at trans people. They were mad at Bud Light for pouring identity politics down their throats at a time when they were already being overserved.

When Dylan Mulvaney unveiled the can, the country was fiercely divided over the issue of biological men competing in women's sports, which I'm in favor of only if I can bet money on it in Vegas. Parents were also battling woke school boards over their plans to push the idea of gender reassignment surgeries to students as young as five.

For my money, we should probably teach kids to add numbers before they learn to subtract their junk, but that doesn't mean I'm anti-trans. It means I'm pro—*Do whatever you want to your body once you're over the age of eighteen.* If you polled beer drinkers, the vast majority would fall under the same umbrella. That being said, I'm not encouraging *anyone* to poll beer drinkers, unless you've got a degree in translating slurred speech, which I highly doubt, because if you did, you'd be working for the Biden administration.

But given how tribal the culture wars have gotten, it's no surprise the move backfired as badly as it did. The exact same thing would have happened on the left if, say, Ben & Jerry's started selling its liberal customers a new flavor called Kid Rocky Road. Or imagine if Subaru started selling a special edition Outback called the Proud Boy. (This would be equally shocking for the mere suggestion that a guy would drive a Subaru.) But if either of these happened there'd be riots at every Whole Foods checkout line in America, which would cause millions of dollars in damages. Or, like, three avocados.

Fortunately for Dylan Mulvaney, the influencer game continues to pay handsomely, even after putting the "can" in "canceled." It's unclear if Bud Light will ever recover its lost status with beer drinkers. At the very least, the story will serve as a lesson to other brewers: This isn't what customers meant when they asked the bartender for a beer and some nuts.

I will show myself all the way out.

James Bond, J.K. Rowling, and Jason Aldean

J.K. Rowling is one of the most successful authors who's ever lived. Her Harry Potter series has sold over 600 million copies, been translated into eighty-four different languages, and inspired eight blockbuster films. Not to mention Broadway plays, video games, and a host of other things this book you're reading will *never* amount to.

The other key difference between me and Rowling is she writes about imaginary wizards, whereas I met a few real ones during my time as a New York City cabdriver.

Oh, buddy!

Anyone who tells you we don't have life on other planets has never spent a twelve-hour shift in a Yellow Cab driving around the hobbits, time travelers, and self-proclaimed ghosts who frequent this town. I've picked up some *real* winners over the years, including a woman who got in with a sock puppet on each hand and proceeded to trash my driving all the way to Brooklyn. To this day, I'm not sure whose audience is more incredulous about this story: mine because I got yelled at by sock puppets, or hers because she claims she met a white cabdriver in New York City? Let's just say we both have our skeptics.

I'm not sure J.K. Rowling has interacted with either of these phenomena, but the one place we do overlap is in our support for biological sex. Granted, she supports it on social media and I support it on websites we can't name in a family-friendly book like this. But the fact remains we've both received some harsh judgments over the years, mine from the tech support guys at Best Buy, hers from the outrage mob online. Yeah, if J.K. Rowling were to write a book about her online discussions of biology, it would likely be titled *Harry Potter and the Bomb Threats*. Man, oh, boy, oh, man, has the cancel crowd tried to blow her off the map.

We begin, as always, on Twitter, this time in December 2019. Over in the UK, a woman named Maya Forstater had just been fired from her job after expressing her belief that it is "impossible to change one's sex."

A judge ruled that Forstater's views were not protected speech under Britain's antidiscrimination laws. After hearing the outcome, J.K. Rowling voiced her support for trans people but took exception to the speech ruling, tweeting:

Dress however you please. Call yourself whatever you like. Sleep with any consenting adult who'll have you. Live your best life in peace and security. But force women out of their jobs for stating that sex is real?

It's a pretty measured take. She's not denying anyone their right to identify or to live however they'd like. She's simply standing up for speech rights we should all have. Unfortunately, the Twitter crowd handles measured takes the way O.J. handles marital disagreements. Within minutes of her tweet, the White Broncos hit the highway in full force.

Rowling was besieged with thousands of angry tweets, many from people who expressed heartbreak that an author they loved so much could be "so intolerant." There were hundreds of videos of people burning Rowling's books, and millions more clicked "like" and "share."

This is why cancel culture as a whole is such an irrational plague on society. She didn't say *Get rid of trans people* or *Shame them into a hole.* She said *this*:

I respect every trans person's right to live any way that feels authentic and comfortable to them. I'd march with you if you were discriminated against on the basis of being trans. At the same time, my life has been shaped by being female. I do not believe it's hateful to say so.

It's hardly the stuff of a homicidal hatemonger, but away we went, because this is how the mob gets their way: by shouting people into forced compliance with their views for fear of being their next victim. And they don't just come after Rowling; they come after her defenders. When there are no more defenders, they come after people who like her books. When no one will admit to liking her books, they threaten to run a 23andMe DNA test on anyone who might be related to someone who's liked them in the past. To put it in Harry Potter terms, the point is to turn their latest societal supervillain into "He or She who must not be named." With that accomplished, they move on to the next outrage.

If we're being rational, there's gotta be a better rallying cry for tolerance than *We need to create a world where* everyone *feels accepted! Unless they disagree with us, in which case, destroy their careers immediately.*

But if being rational were still a thing, there wouldn't *be* an outrage industry.

Rowling's Twitter account got further submerged in the Deathly Hallows a few months later when the Covid pandemic saw the world go clinically insane during lockdowns.

In June 2020, Rowling was presumably bored at home like the rest of us when she read an op-ed that was making the rounds on Twitter titled *"Opinion: Creating a more equal post–COVID-19 world for people who menstruate."*

Her response:

"People who menstruate." I'm sure there used to be a word for those people. Someone help me out. Wumben? Wimpund? Woomud?

Eighty-one thousand people *liked* Rowling's tweet because it turns out not everybody in the world is on board with erasing biological women. Yet Rowling was labeled a TERF, which stands for a "Trans Exclusionary Radical Feminist."

Incredibly, all of this happened while the *Oxford Dictionary* defined the word "menstruation" as "the process in a woman of discharging blood and other material from the lining of the uterus at intervals of about one lunar month from puberty until the menopause, except during pregnancy."

If you're wondering why nobody wanted to cancel the dictionary for saying only women menstruate, check out the vocabularies of the people rage-tweeting at Rowling. Let's just say if they do own a dictionary, it's a little dusty.

Rowling went on to tweet:

If sex isn't real, there's no same-sex attraction. If sex isn't real the lived reality of women globally is erased. I know and love trans people but removing the concept of sex removes the ability of many people to meaningfully discuss their lives. It isn't hate to speak the truth.

Two hundred ten thousand people liked this tweet because, again, Rowling wasn't saying *Ban trans people* or *Don't be friends with them.* She was simply using her massive platform to push back against an outrage mob that pistol-whips people into playing along. Standing up for her beliefs doesn't make her hateful; it makes her heroic. Because she realizes that if the top-selling author of our lifetime can't feel safe speaking out, what chance do regular people like you and me have?

I don't want to get this book bogged down in a debate about menstruation. My editor is having enough trouble with my ability to use periods.

But everyone, whether you love J.K. Rowling or you're using her books as firewood, needs to understand that tolerance does not mean *Share our worldview* or else.

To quote that pesky *Oxford Dictionary* again, "tolerance" is described as "the ability or willingness to tolerate something, in particular the existence of opinions or behavior that one does not necessarily agree with."

Apparently, nobody read this page to Daniel Radcliffe, because the man who played Harry Potter in the movies tried to put a spell on J.K. Rowling's Twitter account. With the mob going full Dumbledore, Radcliffe amplified the controversy even more by condemning her comments to his millions of followers:

Transgender women are women. Any statement to the contrary erases the identity and dignity of transgender people and goes against all advice given by professional health associations who have far more knowledge on the subject matter than Jo [Rowling] or I.

Radcliffe went on to apologize to the trans community for the "hurt and pain" caused by Rowling's comments, and to further distance himself from the feeding frenzy he highlighted his own work on a charity that tries to reduce the suicide rate among LGBTQ kids.

Look. As a Knicks fan, I applaud anyone who wants to reduce suicide rates. But I think we could help vulnerable people in the trans community *a lot* more if folks like Daniel Radcliffe stopped disingenuously telling them that every disagreement is a form of hatred. It can't be good for the morale of vulnerable people to constantly be told that the world wants them dead. And there's also the fact that it's patently not true. Not even a little.

Speaking as a guy who hosts a three-hour radio show every day with millions of conservative listeners who've spent zillions of hours discussing these headlines, my message for the trans community would be this: Yes, we have some major differences of opinion on biological men playing in women's sports and having babies.

That being said, none of my listeners are being told that you don't have a right to exist or that they should hate you. Unless of course you're one of those people who talks on speakerphone in public, in which case nobody likes you, and not because of your identity but because you're being an inconsiderate a**hole.

The cancel crowd loves to categorize everything as hate because it makes it harder to disagree with them. It might be good for their leverage, but the constant drumbeat of doom can't be helping anyone else.

To her credit, J.K. Rowling has continued to stand her biological ground. Daniel Radcliffe has continued to embrace the magic side of the issue, but what's crazy is that a decade ago there wouldn't have been an issue for them to disagree on.

Throughout all of history, the world believed that only women can give birth, so much so that it became a frequent source of comedy to say otherwise. Monty Python did a legendary bit in their 1979 film, *Life of Brian*, in which a man is called delusional for declaring that he's going to start calling himself a woman and having babies.

Noted liberal Sacha Baron Cohen dedicated an entire episode of *Who Is America* to what was considered in 2018 to be a pretend belief that men could get pregnant. The sketch was punctuated with him delivering something called an "ass baby." The jokes worked because we'd never contemplated how or where a baby would come out of if a man did give birth, nor just how awkward the process might get.

There were no calls to cancel Monty Python in '79 or Sacha Baron Cohen in '18. Nor were there any calls to cancel Mister Rogers over the course of the '60s, '70s, '80s, and '90s as he once sang about gender on his hit song "Everybody's Fancy."

The lyrics in verse two begin:

"Boys are boys from the beginning. / Girls are girls right from the start. / If you were born a girl, you'll stay a girl. / And grow up to be a lady."

Just when you thought he couldn't get any more bigoted or violent, he tacked on verse three:

"Only girls can be the mommies. / Only boys can be the daddies."

Rogers released the song in 1967 and continued to sing it everywhere he went during his career, including an appearance on the *Tonight Show* in September 1980.

Mister Rogers was not considered a bigoted hate machine. He was an American icon whose life was portrayed in film by Tom frickin' Hanks, who's not exactly from the wrong side of society's train tracks either. If Fred Rogers sang this song today, he'd be "Mister Canceled" and he'd be lucky if he could be played by "Tom from MySpace," let alone Tom Hanks.

Why? Because the left loves mischaracterizing disagreement as calls to violence, mainly because it forces society to give them their way.

Everyone needs to renounce their speech rights and agree with us or people will die!

It's a great way to wage a social pressure campaign, but it's a terrible way to have a productive discussion when our positions are so far apart. My point is: Yes, liberals suddenly believe that men can have babies, and conservatives continue to believe the truth. But it doesn't mean we can't all believe there's great value in "agreeing to disagree" and chilling the fuck out.

James Bond author Ian Fleming was not taking his chances on the outrage mob chilling out. Apparently, their ongoing war on all speech new and old left him "shaken *and* stirred." Okay, I'll stop the Bond puns before I get poked in the eye by a Goldfinger.

In February 2023, Ian Fleming Publications Ltd announced that James Bond novels were going to be reissued with a number of racial references removed. The new print run was to coincide with the seventieth anniversary of Fleming's first novel, *Casino Royale*. Apparently, Bond didn't want to roll the dice on the mob dumping a martini all over his fancy-ass tux.

So, in addition to the freshly edited text, the new books now have the following disclaimer at the front:

"This book was written at a time when terms and attitudes which might be considered offensive by modern readers were commonplace. A number of updates have been made in this edition, while keeping as close as possible to the original text and the period in which it is set."

The fact that no one was calling for these changes but Fleming's estate announced them anyway shows you just how pervasive the outrage mob has become in our society.

This was not the work of a guy who found Jesus a little late in the service. *Casino Royale* was written in 1953, so by 2023 Fleming had long since left the Church, bought a few brownies at the bake sale, and went home to watch football on the couch with his hand down his pants like Al Bundy. (At least, that's how I picture it.)

In fact, he died in 1964. But his relatives, who have happily cashed royalty checks for *sixty years,* are now repenting for his sins, because they know there are thousands of people reviewing old texts in an effort to gin up some controversy. His publishers wanted to fireproof their big reissue against such a thing, so they self-canceled his words lest they run the risk of having their big sales push overshadowed by a Twitter trend that could leave them #bankrupt.

I can't defend Fleming's use of the N-word in the '50s—or any decade for that matter. The only edit I took exception to was a scene in *Live and Let Die.* Bond was visiting a nightclub in Harlem, and the publishers removed Fleming's reference to the fact that "Bond could hear the audience panting and grunting like pigs at the trough."

Folks, anyone who thinks that Black people are the only ones who can sound like pigs has never been to one of my mom's Sunday dinner parties.

If you ask me (which you didn't, but I'll weigh in anyway because it's my book), leaving offensive terms in old texts is representative of the progress we've made on race in society. The fact that you read something and it jumps out at you means you're now living in a standard that's evolved *quite* a long way.

That being said, I am *not* gonna die on this hill. I have zero desire to use the N-word. Nor do I have any right to use it, because I'm not a rapper. But here's a pro tip on that one: if you are a white person who happens to be doing karaoke, you should still NEVER use the N-word. Especially if it's not in the original lyrics. That one could backfire big-time.

Nobody knows more about musical backfires than the folks who tried to cancel Jason Aldean's country smash "Try That in a Small Town." The song was released in May 2023, but it wasn't until July that Aldean released the accompanying video, filled with real footage of the chaos that's taken place in our streets over the past few years. It showed violent riots from the summer of 2020 in which protesters looted stores, attacked police, and set towns on fire. There were lots of shots in which masked criminals assaulted people and *shot* them.

With the pandemonium playing behind him, Aldean sang the lyrics:

Sucker punch somebody on a sidewalk
Carjack an old lady at a red light
Pull a gun on the owner of a liquor store
Ya think it's cool, well, act a fool if ya like . . .

Well, try that in a small town
See how far you make it down the road
Around here, we take care of our own

You may not support songs about vigilante justice, but it's worth pointing out that there's only a market for them because in the past four years the country has often looked like it needed some.

Meaning, he's up there singing the equivalent of "Bring It On,

Fuckers," because everybody knows there's a ton of fuckers out there terrorizing innocent people.

We've all seen a major quality-of-life decline in liberal cities that started with them literally being set on fire in the summer of 2020. My word.

New York is *terrible* right now! We used to have these famous "walking tours," where you check out all the old, fancy architecture. We still have them, but they're now called *running tours*, because you're usually getting chased.

Aldean seemed to be saying that crime is harder to pull off in smaller communities where they have civic pride and everyone knows each other.

The left tried to spin it as a racist ode to lynchings, which Tennessee state representative Justin Jones said in calling it "an attempt to normalize racist [*sic*], violence, vigilantism and white nationalism."

What's crazy is that for all this talk about racism in the song, Aldean never mentioned it in any of the lyrics. Yet, for some reason, liberals assume that saying you're anti-crime means you must also be anti-Black. It sounds like they're the ones who have low opinions of the Black community.

It's a point that was brilliantly made on my radio show by a Black comedian named Charles McBee. If you're not familiar with his work, Charles was the head writer for Charlamagne Tha God's show on Comedy Central, *Hell of a Week*.

If you recall, it was Charlamagne who had Hillary Clinton on his morning radio show, *The Breakfast Club*, during the 2016 election when she infamously claimed she carried a bottle of hot sauce in her purse. To this day, I'm not sure how it fit in there with the private email server. Apparently, Charlamagne wasn't buying it, either, because he told her she was only saying it to pander to the Black community.

Like Charlamagne, Charles is a super-sharp dude who sees through a lot of the race pandering that goes on by the left. The day the Aldean story broke, we had him on the radio, and I'll never forget his opening line, because it crystallizes so many of the backlashes of our times:

ME: Charles McBee joins us now on *Fox Across America*.
CHARLES: What's up, man? I must confess, I didn't really have time to read up on this Jason Aldean story yet. Can you please tell me who the white liberals are telling Black folks to be mad at now?

That's the "Small Town" controversy in a nutshell. White Democrats trying to spread division and hatred by slandering Republicans as racists.

But in the case of Jason Aldean, as McBee pointed out on the show, this left-wing claim that Black people don't also take great pride in their small-town communities speaks to a much greater racial ignorance on the left's part.

I couldn't agree more, but history will show that the people at Country Music Television don't follow my lead—which is crazy, given how many badass Western shirts I've worn on TV over the years. CMT pulled the video after a wave of negative critiques rolled in on its YouTube feed. From there, every liberal commentator on cable began referring to "Small Town" as a musical celebration of the Klan.

Rolling Stone slammed it for "this narrative of white nationalism." And other members of the music business gave Aldean the business as well, including Sheryl Crow, who tweeted:

There's nothing small-town or American about promoting violence. You should know that better than anyone having survived a mass shooting.

This is not American or small town-like. It's just lame.

Go ahead and preach it, girl! But, please, don't ever try to Soak Up the Sun in a blue city without bringing extra security. Take it from a guy who's been jumped in his taxi on the way through Central Park. Driving that route was not My Favorite Mistake. Although it's correct to say the First Cut Was the Deepest.

But it wasn't just music stars who peaked in the '90s coming after Aldean. The criticisms even spread outside the entertainment industry to places where people go to get tortured, like MSNBC.

Yet, in what can only be described as the biggest backfire in cancel culture history, the song shot all the way up to number one on the *Billboard* charts. Conservatives started buying it as a middle finger to the mob and boosted its visibility, at which point other music fans jumped onto the cause. Think about *that*. The song came out in May and lay dormant on the charts for two months until one day of attempted cancels took it all the way to the top.

It's pretty hilarious to watch the backfire, but at the same time it really does speak to a dangerous divide in our society.

We should all be looking out for the law-abiding citizens of every race who are being terrorized by the violence in our cities. And while the song undoubtedly skyrocketed up the charts because of conservatives, the truth is nobody in either political party wants to live someplace where crime is out of control.

Which is why it would seriously help if the members of Club Outrage started getting madder at violent criminals than the guys who sing about stopping them. I understand Aldean's message isn't for everyone, but trust me: you'd rather get cornered by a guy with a guitar than a guy with a gun any day of the week.

Unless the guy with the guitar is in a Dave Matthews cover band.

Relax, Dave Matthews fans. I wasn't insulting you or your favorite band. In writing that C-plus joke I simply picked an artist whose fans are way too stoned to come after me.

After all, I've got enough potential attackers because I live in a Big Town.

Kelly Files

R. Kelly was the top-selling male R&B artist of the '90s, selling over 60 million albums in that decade alone. He was also big on streaming, but enough about his sex life.

Forgive me for taking it here, but the singer with a ton of gold records was said to be a fan of golden showers. If you don't know what that is, I congratulate you on being a decent person. Rather than having you google it and ruin your hard drive, let's just say there are multiple reasons he's known as the Number One singer.

Yes, this is lowbrow terrain we've entered, even for this book, so I won't dwell on it any longer. Long, disgusting story short: The man who wrote "Your Body's Callin'" received a collect call from cancel culture in 2019. Most people would argue it was long overdue, given his propensity for odd fetishes and underage women.

To recap: in 1994, Kelly married the late R&B singer Aaliyah during a secret ceremony, but the marriage was annulled a few months later because she was fifteen at the time of the wedding. Everyone knew something was off when the minister said, "You may *not* kiss the bride." In 1996, Kelly was sued by a high school student over an alleged affair that began when he was twenty-four and she was fifteen. Kelly settled with the aspiring singer for $250,000, but to put it in music terms, his troubles were just turning the Ignition.

In December 2000, the *Chicago Sun-Times* cited court records and interviews alleging that Kelly "used his position of fame and influence as a pop superstar to meet girls as young as 15 and have sex with them."

This squared with a follow-up piece the *Sun-Times* ran in 2002 in which music critic Jim DeRogatis claimed to have anonymously received a twenty-nine-minute videotape allegedly showing Kelly having sex with a minor.

That news broke on the same day Kelly performed at the opening ceremonies of the Winter Olympics in Salt Lake City. As a ski announcer might say, it was all downhill from there.

Kelly was indicted on child pornography charges in 2002 over evidence stemming from the reports in the *Chicago Sun-Times*. The case didn't go to trial for another five years, but during that time his wife filed for an order of protection for alleged physical abuse. He ultimately won acquittal on all eight charges in 2008, but his victims would later testify that he did so by bribing their families and making threats to keep them from cooperating with prosecutors. His wife filed for divorce a year after his acquittal, but most of his fans stuck with him as he went on multiple tours and even released a greatest-hits album titled *Playlist: The Very Best of R. Kelly* in 2010.

But whatever goodwill Kelly possessed in mainstream society evaporated overnight in January 2019 with the release of a Lifetime docuseries called *Surviving R. Kelly*.

The multi-episode event chronicled the tales of his underage victims, but all it took was one airing for the cancel navy to sink his battleship.

Up until then, Kelly had managed to keep his proclivities On the Down Low, as his song goes. Sure, there were trials and lawsuits, but his public image remained intact enough for him to sell out arenas and perform alongside some of the biggest names in music.

He released a duet with Lady Gaga in 2013, and he received six more Grammy nominations, including one for a duet with Jennifer Hudson in a 2014 song called "It's Your World." It wasn't his best work, but apparently music fans were just happy to see him with women over eighteen.

All of that changed when 2 million people watched the debut episode of *Surviving R. Kelly*, which transformed him into a serial abuser overnight in the eyes of the public.

Now, to be clear, people are *always* upset when they watch Lifetime movies. I'm pretty sure that's the hook: it's like a TV dominatrix for women who want to feel like hell. Abusive husbands, terminally ill neighbors—it doesn't end well for anybody in those films, least of all the viewers.

The documentary left people next-level disturbed, because unlike Lifetime's usual little shops of household horrors, the series didn't feature actors. It depicted real victims recounting their abuses at the height of the #MeToo movement.

Accusers said he kept them as sex slaves, locked in his home with no access to their families or the outside world. They claimed he groomed young men and women who were aspiring singers and recorded the sex acts he forced them to perform. He was also said to have locked them in rooms without food or access to a bathroom for days.

Twitter had sentenced Kelly to life in prison by the end of episode one, and that was enough for Lady Gaga to issue an apology for working with him in the first place. She also had their duet pulled off streaming services. His record Label, RCA, also jumped on the cancel train and severed ties with Kelly in the days after the series premiered.

Things got worse when the lawyer who won him acquittal in the 2008 child pornography case told the *Chicago Sun-Times* the singer was "guilty as hell." The public backlash was intense enough to inspire investigators to take a fresh look into Kelly's deviant past, and in February 2019 he was arrested in Cook County, Illinois, on ten counts of aggravated criminal sexual abuse.

Kelly was released on $100,000 bail. I would imagine it had to be hard for his lawyer to argue he wasn't a flight risk, knowing the guy sang "I Believe I Can Fly."

Federal prosecutors in New York also cuffed Kelly weeks later, but he maintained his innocence in a widely televised interview with Gayle King that was truly unforgettable, although everyone who watched it tried. There were a lot of wild rants and teary-eyed claims that only convinced the public of one thing: he had to go into singing because he would never have made it as an actor.

Shortly after the interview, the Philadelphia City Council passed a resolution to keep the singer from performing there. That might have been a gift to Kelly, given the conditions in Philly these days, but it wasn't just American cities pulling the plug. Germany also rescinded its invite to a concert that was scheduled for later that year, and this one really got my attention. You know it's bad when the country that supported David Hasselhoff's music career won't have you.

Spotify wouldn't have him either. A trending hashtag called #Mute-RKelly inspired the streaming giant to stop promoting his music and featuring it on playlists. iTunes followed suit the same week, in effect canceling any chance he had at topping the charts ever again.

Don't cry for R. Kelly; cry for his victims, because he was convicted in multiple jurisdictions on charges of child pornography, racketeering, and sex trafficking. The judges sentenced him to a combined thirty-one years in prison, which is slightly shorter than his video for "Trapped in the Closet."

If you didn't see it, it's like the Oregon Trail of music videos. People you start watching it with run out of food and die by the time you get to the end.

Not R. Kelly, though. This guy has three hot meals coming his way courtesy of the state for the next three decades. His music is no longer promoted, but it does remain popular online, which has sparked fierce debates over what to do with the content of canceled artists.

Do you keep it available on the major platforms? Or do you banish it to someplace no one with decent musical taste would ever go, like a Jessica Simpson concert?

In Kelly's case it wasn't just the outrage mob who took him down. It was the cops. Cancel culture meets handcuff culture. But even so, he wasn't the first music star to face the music.

Phil Spector was convicted of murder, and every album he produced is available to this day. Chris Brown was arrested for assaulting Rihanna after the 2009 Grammy Awards, only to come back and win a Grammy three years later for his album *F.A.M.E.* (This should give hope to Will Smith fans.)

The late rapper Tupac Shakur was convicted of sexual assault in 1995 and served eleven months before being bailed out by producer Suge Knight. It's worth noting that Suge Knight is now serving twenty-eight years in prison after pleading guilty to voluntary manslaughter charges stemming from a 2015 hit-and-run attack.

The point I'm trying to make is that if you stopped playing the music, movies, and comedy of everyone who exhibited deviant behavior, we'd be facing a major content shortage that could inspire a full-on societal collapse, given people's addiction to staring at screens all day.

Sure, they could put down their devices and go outside, but that could only lead to them interacting with other untethered people who'd act in unpredictable ways. And let's face it, if Americans really wanted to spend more time with the mentally ill, Joy Reid's show would have much higher ratings.

For my money, separating the art from the artist and enjoying a song by a problematic person is not an endorsement of their behavior. For instance, you don't listen to R. Kelly sing "Bump and Grind" because you like underage women. Well, you might if you're Prince Andrew.

As for the rest of us, I think the reason we love certain songs is because they not only appeal to our musical sensibilities but they transport us back to more innocent times in our lives and the artists' lives too.

When I listen to Michael Jackson's "Thriller," it's like time traveling back to an era when I spent ten hours a day watching MTV—which might also explain my report cards from those years. To this day, the second the song comes on, I remember being totally freaked out by the werewolf and the zombie people and the haunting voice-over by Vincent Price. Although based on what we know today, the most shocking part of the "Thriller" video was that Michael Jackson had a girlfriend.

But the point is the point: nothing that brings you joy should be canceled from your own private life, assuming it's legal and not being done at the expense of anybody else's well-being. Sure, the publishers made me include the last half of that sentence, but the fact remains, we should all retain the right to make our own decision based on our relationship with the content.

I was never a big R. Kelly fan, but if his music offers you an escape from the torments of everyday life, my advice is to press "play" if you're not distracted by his reality.

Sure, he's a monster who's serving thirty-one years in prison, but his songs didn't abuse anyone. He did. And I think we're only being honest if we acknowledge the nuance of the situation. Yes, for some people, listening to R. Kelly's tracks can still bring them joy. While for others, he's peed it all away.

Logos, Lincoln, and Live PD

The summer of 2020 was cancel culture's Super Bowl. The entire country had gone mad from Covid lockdowns and went madder after the murder of George Floyd a few months later.

Yes, America was rightfully outraged by the video. No, America was not in a good mental place after being trapped inside for three months of death counts and day drinking. I'm not sure how you handled house arrest, but you know your boozing was getting bad if you got thrown out of a Zoom cocktail party.

George Floyd's death lit the fuse on an emotional powder keg that exploded into every aspect of society and made *anything* a cancel target at a time when mobs were looting real Targets. Things got so crazy at one point that a San Francisco school board was exploring the idea of removing Abraham Lincoln's name from one of its high schools.

Abraham Lincoln!

This one hit home for me because my son is named Lincoln. I gotta be honest: I never, in a billion years, thought it would be controversial to name my kid after the guy who *freed the slaves*. But from now on, just to be safe, whenever we're in California he goes by his middle name, O.J.

The school board ultimately decided to keep our sixteenth president's name on the building—not that students knew, because they remained locked out for another year. Which brings me to my larger point about the stupidity of mob mentalities and cancel culture as a whole:

They're almost always fighting the wrong battles. Even when they are standing up for great causes, like protecting the Black community, the burn-it-all-down mentality of cancel culture never fixes anything.

For instance, the Defund the Police movement championed by liberal activists like AOC led to a series of budget cuts that crushed morale on the force and sent violent crime rates soaring in major cities along the way. Although I'm not gonna pick on AOC, because this is a woman who's so dumb she studied for a Covid test (and then assumed the two lines meant she was having twins).

Even the other changes made that summer, like canceling TV shows and syrup logos, have done nothing to boost test scores for kids trapped in failing inner-city schools.

When you're living in a country where one in three schoolkids isn't learning at a grade level, making sure they don't put Aunt Jemima syrup on their pancakes doesn't seem like the right place to start the turnaround. But there we were, watching the cancel crowd give Aunt Jemima a pink slip.

This one got going after a TikTok user posted a video called "How to Cook Breakfast Without Being Racist." The narrator claimed Aunt

Jemima has been reinforcing racial stereotypes since she debuted 130 years ago. On a superficial level, I had no idea Aunt Jemima had been around that long, but it's true. As you read this, she's now 134. Same age as Mitch McConnell.

I don't know that the vast majority of Americans thought of Aunt Jemima as something out of a minstrel show or considered eating pancakes an endorsement of such things. But Quaker Oats, which produces Aunt Jemima syrup, wasn't taking any chances at a time when mobs were taking rocks and throwing them through storefront windows.

In June 2020 the company's vice president of marketing, Kristin Kroepfl, released a statement saying:

"We recognize Aunt Jemima's origins are based on a racial stereotype. As we work to make progress toward racial equality through several initiatives, we also must take a hard look at our portfolio of brands and ensure they reflect our values and meet our consumers' expectations."

Now, to be clear, the logo had been fine with their "values and consumers' expectations" for the previous 130 years. There was no outcry, no call for a racial reckoning, which means nothing she said in that statement was reflective of anything other than a desire to be on the right side of the rage sweeping the country. It was performative allyship designed to align their brand with the trendy political narrative that America was systemically racist and this was everyone's moment to step up.

Forget the fact that we were living in the most tolerant and inclusive society in history. Completely disregard the reality that white supremacist nations don't traditionally make a habit of electing a Black president twice. You never let the facts get in the way of a good riot.

This is the danger of social pressure campaigns: once they get rolling at the corporate level, it becomes a game of virtue-signaling dominoes, and every piece that falls reinforces the mob mentality as being correct.

To wit, just hours after Aunt Jemima got the heave-ho, Mars

announced that it was time to send Uncle Ben's rice off to that big grocery store shelf in the sky.

Their statement:

"Racism has no place in society. We stand in solidarity with the Black community, our Associates and our partners in the fight for social justice. We know to make the systemic change needed, it's going to take a collective effort from all of us—individuals, communities and organizations of all sizes around the world."

For those of you who don't speak "corporate pandering," it's worth noting that up until then Uncle Ben's origins were not considered racist. According to the company's website, "Uncle Ben" was inspired by a Texas farmer who was known in the region for growing excellent rice. He wasn't a slave and neither was the Black man on the box who portrayed him. Frank Brown was a waiter at the Chicago restaurant where the company's co-founders hatched the idea to call the company Uncle Ben's, and they hired Brown to portray their namesake.

So understand that the models and their families got paid from these companies, which means the cancel crowd conceivably took away an income stream from Black families in the name of . . . equality?

There has never been a dumber time to be alive.

The third brand to get trampled in this stampede of stupidity was Mrs. Butterworth's syrup. Shortly after the store manager showed Aunt Jemima and Uncle Ben to the automatic door, Conagra Brands announced a full packaging review for Mrs. Butterworth, who, according to the company website, debuted in 1961.

The company stated that, at the time, the bottle was meant to evoke the image of a loving grandmother making breakfast for the family. Fast-forward through *six decades* of no one having a problem with it and a spokesman was now saying in a statement "the company recognizes that it may be perceived differently."

Which is the board recognizing that it's safer to signal your obedience to the mob than it is to try and escape your corporate headquarters after it's been set on fire.

For me, the craziest part is that, to this day, none of us even knows if Derek Chauvin killed George Floyd because of the color of his skin. He wasn't charged with a hate crime. All we really know is that he was a thug cop that we absolutely needed to get rid of. Thankfully, the system worked in convicting him, because everyone who watched that horrific video agreed he belonged in jail.

What we didn't agree on was the violent backlash that followed. Conservatives bashed the lawlessness at every turn. Left-wing networks went out of their way to frame the chaos as "no big deal" because they didn't want it to hurt their party's chances on Election Day. That summer's riots caused over $10 billion in property damage and led to dozens of deaths as the rioters were emboldened by weak-kneed corporations and race-baiting politicians eager to convert this rage into votes in that fall's election.

The liberal media's mantra in the summer of 2020 seemed to be *So what if they just burned down a Little Caesars? These folks will vote Democrat if we cheer them on!*

On the plus side, this is the first time a Little Caesars pizza was fully cooked. The minus is that trust in media may never recover from a CNN banner describing a riot in Kenosha, Wisconsin, as "fiery but mostly peaceful protests." Those flames all over the screen at the time not only engulfed a few businesses, but we are sad to report that objective truth also checked out that night. There was little fanfare, as it had been on life support at CNN for quite some time.

Fiery but *mostly* peaceful!

If CNN was around in 1912, it would've described the *Titanic*'s maiden voyage as "watery but mostly iceberg-free."

With the election looming *big* in the fall, there was a constant battle that summer to assign blame for the chaos, with left-wing pundits blaming America as a whole and quoting Dr. Martin Luther King Jr., who famously said, "A riot is the language of the unheard."

To which conservatives like myself responded, "If people in the inner cities are having a problem feeling heard, we should probably start by asking why the liberals who've run these places the past fifty years aren't listening?"

Look, pal, bud, friend. The truth is I honestly don't know how to address you because I thought it was a little early in the book to have the *What are we?* talk. Hell, I don't even have your pronouns yet.

But speaking as your undefined reading companion, I can tell you with absolute certainty that there were, in fact, millions of good-hearted protesters who took to the streets hoping to change things for the better. And they were right to demand that bad cops be held accountable. But the anarchists and race-baiting politicians who tried to make the case that there weren't any good cops couldn't have been more disingenuous . . . or deadly.

Yet that's exactly what the mob did in the summer of 2020. TV shows like *Live PD* and *Cops* were taken off the air because we couldn't have anything that portrayed police in a positive light. At one point there was even a push for Nickelodeon to cancel a *cartoon police dog* on the show *PAW Patrol*, the claim being that "Chase" reinforced the "good cop stereotype" and might trick kids into thinking cops were okay.

Fortunately, Chase the Dog hung on to the gig—mainly because liberals realized that if society was gonna start ditching characters who were led around on a leash and sniffed everyone they passed, that would eliminate Joe Biden.

All of this anti-cop chaos built to the cancel crescendo of Democratic squad members like Congresswomen Ilhan Omar, AOC, and Cori Bush flat out calling for the *defunding of police*.

Now, I don't mean to get all serious on you, but it cannot be emphasized enough just how spectacularly stupid it was for politicians to endorse this idea.

Police of all colors are doing the single most important job in our society. It also happens to be the most difficult. In a lot of ways, they're like the NFL referees of life in that they make millions of split-second decisions each week and we only talk about the calls we don't like, the key difference being that NFL refs don't make decisions that have life-

and-death consequences. Well, they might if you gamble as much as I did in my twenties.

The smartphone era has allowed us to pass judgment on police as we review their behavior millions of emotional miles removed from the adrenaline they feel in the heat of a violent altercation. It rarely gives us the full scope of the challenge they face in a given situation, but even so, if we see something as egregiously terrible as we did with Derek Chauvin, then, yes, we should be all in on convicting a bad cop. Going forward, we'd be wise to show *a lot* more grace and support to the good cops than we did in the summer of 2020 because we need them more than ever.

You cannot have a society without law and order. Forget school, forget shopping, and forget every pro sporting event where police are protested as they're simultaneously counted on to keep everyone safe. Cops were even being assigned to protect the idiots who were spitting on them and calling them pigs in the summer of 2020.

I don't know that I've lived through anything more embarrassing for our country, and I say that as a guy who saw *both* of the *Sex and the City* sequels.

Sadly, in the summer of 2020, dozens of Democrats helped push this vile anti-cop narrative that led to major cities like New York and Los Angeles cutting police budgets under the delusion that cops posed a threat to the community. The plan was to rely more heavily on social workers who could defuse situations before they escalated but anyone with an eighth of a brain threw the challenge flag on that call. Let's face it, you're never going to find yourself getting attacked and yell out, "Somebody call a social worker!"

No, when the game is on the line, you're always going to pick the boys in blue over the persons with the blue hair.

Thankfully, the left received enough pushback from all sides on the defund movement and ultimately updated their position to claim "de-funding" would simply mean taking *some* of the police budget. Which doesn't make it any better, because in the end nobody benefits from having fewer cops around, and even the Democrats pushing the defund movement agree with me.

We know this because weeks after she began pushing the defund movement, Missouri congresswoman Cori Bush was outed for spending over $200,000 on an armed security detail to guard her everywhere she went.

I'm not a weatherman, but if I had to guess, the forecast in her district calls for high levels of hypocrisy. Must be from all that global whining. I say so because when she was busted for employing cops, she responded with a word salad of ridiculous complaints:

> *I have private security because my body is worth being on this planet right now. I have private security because they, the white supremacist racist narrative that they drive into this country. The fact that they don't care that this Black woman that has put her life on the line, they can't match my energy first of all.*
>
> *This Black woman who puts her life on the line. They don't care that I could be taken out of here. They actually probably are OK with that, but this is the thing: I won't let them get that off. You can't get that off. I'm going to make sure I have security because I know I have had attempts on my life and I have too much work to do. There are too many people that need help right now for me to allow that.*
>
> *So if I end up spending $200,000, if I spend 10, 10, 10 more dollars on it, you know what, I get to be here to do the work. So suck it up and defunding the police has to happen. We need to defund the police and put that money into social safety nets because we're trying to save lives.*

To be clear, getting rid of cops would stop violence the way getting rid of brakes would stop cars. The idea of doing either is criminally stupid. But if Bush truly believes the country is so racist that a Black woman like her *must have* security, how could she possibly be okay with taking cops away from the millions of Black women who can't afford armed guards? And if we really are *that* racist, how did she get elected in the first place? And lastly, if cops as a whole are as evil as she says, why is she paying them to *protect* her?

Oddly enough, there's not a single social worker on Bush's protection team.

In fact, anti-gun Cori Bush loves her gun-carrying security team so much that she married one of them in February 2023. Now, granted, he may consider this an act of vengeance after they've been together a few years, but the point is we are living in the death of shame, where politicians have never been happier to push policies they themselves will never have to live with.

It's no different than when the Gavin Newsoms and Nancy Pelosis of the world praised lockdowns, only to get caught going out on the town. It turns out that when Democrats said, "We're all in this together," by "this" they meant the bar at the French Laundry. But when it comes to society's need for law and order, we absolutely are all in this one as a team.

The good news is everyone wants bad cops off the streets. But the abandoning of good cops that took place in the summer of 2020 has led to all kinds of chaos in the communities that count on them the most.

It was only possible because of the power wielded by the outrage mob to force gutless politicians and cancel-happy corporations into supporting an anti-cop, anti-American narrative that they *had to know* wasn't good for anybody.

Consider that I once set the Yellow Cab record for the most times getting pulled over by the NYPD in a single shift. But eight tickets and $2,000 in fines later, even I went home that night knowing that we *have to* support the police.

I actually took the NYPD admission test when I was younger, and the truth is I would have been a cop if it weren't for this thing called a "background check."

Once I heard they'd be looking into the drunken debauchery of my twenties, I politely got the hell out of there and never returned their calls again. Which is exactly what we should do the next time some shameless politician tells us to defund the police.

Mascot Mayhem

If you asked most Americans, they'd tell you the most offensive thing about the Washington Redskins name is the word "Washington." Not to go off on a big crazy political tangent, but if the current members of our government were a football team, the only thing emptier than the stadium would be the promises they made on the campaign trail.

Which is why guys like me have always found the idea of changing Native American mascots to be ridiculous on so many levels. For one thing, it does nothing to address the real issues facing the Native

American community, such as higher rates of alcoholism and heart disease and lower life expectancy.

Seriously, is switching up the halftime show going to help any tribes live longer lives?

No.

Although, to be fair, if they've got season tickets in Washington, they're probably willing to die sooner.

Yeah, the renamed Washington Commanders aren't exactly setting the world on fire. But in the summer of 2020, when rioters were setting their city on fire, the team's owner, Daniel Snyder, announced plans to retire the name out of sensitivity to the Native American community.

Which raises a very serious question: How does this actually help them? Yes, left-wing activists had been complaining about that logo for years, but *no*, changing it does not constitute a tangible quality of life improvement in any way. It's all "slactivism," which allows the people who pressured Washington to feel like they accomplished something. But like the cancellation of Aunt Jemima and Mrs. Butterworth's before it, changing the Redskins name is nothing more than a symbolic gesture masquerading as progress on behalf of people who could use it.

The other reason I'm throwing the challenge flag is because the truth is no team has ever chosen a Native American logo out of mockery for that culture.

Think about it: you don't call yourselves the Kansas City Chiefs because you want your players to be laughed at when they run on the field. You do it as an homage to the men who led some of the fiercest fighting forces the country has ever seen.

You name your team the Chiefs because there's a *pride* that comes with calling yourself a Chief. And if you don't believe me, ask Elizabeth Warren.

When the Atlanta Braves put a hatchet on their jerseys and do the "tomahawk chop," they're not glorifying violence either. If they really wanted fans to associate their team with physical attacks, they'd call themselves the "Real Housewives of Atlanta."

Every name that's ever been chosen was done so because the team thought players and fans could take pride in cheering for it.

Whether you're a Golden State Warrior, a Chicago Blackhawk, or a Cleveland Indian, there's a reverence for your likeness that lends itself to the campiness of sporting events.

None of this was ever meant to be taken seriously, because the whole point of going to a ball game was to *escape* the obligation to take life seriously. You're there to battle the other team, not some friendless activist poser who thinks he's an authority on Native Americans because he streamed the first season of *Yellowstone*.

Talk about a buzzkill.

From the day professional sports commenced, everything happening in the stadiums has been intentionally tongue-in-cheek.

We don't actually line up in battle formations and attack the other fans when the stadium organ plays "Charge!"

Well, you do if you're a Philadelphia fan.

Sporting events have always lent themselves to ridiculousness by design. There are guys in frankfurter costumes running a race around the outfield during the seventh-inning stretch of Major League Baseball games. Is that an accurate depiction of German history? Sadly, no.

"Chief Wahoo" was over-the-top on purpose, not because they wanted to mock the culture but because nobody ever treated pretend things as real up until this age of incentivized grievance we call modern life.

A ball game was supposed to be everyone's chance to not give a shit about anything.

> Take me out to the ball game,
> Take me out to the crowd;
> Buy me some peanuts and Cracker Jack,
> I don't care if I never get back . . .

Yes, it sounds like socialism to charge everybody else for your items at the concession stand, but even so, the guy who wrote the song was so happy to escape the torments of everyday life that he didn't care if he *never* got back. This man was willing to *die* in that stadium! (And he might if they were playing in Chicago.)

But stick with me, dammit!

The Notre Dame Fighting Irish logo literally depicts a drunken Irishman with his hands up in a fighting position, reinforcing every major stereotype about the Irish. But there's never been a real protest because we always knew football logos don't actually affect our lives, plus none of my Irish relatives have time to protest when the beer stand is open. The reason logos that were acceptable for one hundred years suddenly become mortally offensive is because social media has created a world where what you say is way more important than the things you do. Empathy has become a brand instead of an actual character trait. Calling this stuff out might make you feel like a hero but you don't actually save anyone's day; you simply collect some "likes" and move on.

Which is why the NFL has stopped saying the word "Redskins" but the Twitter users who demanded it are yet to start helping Native Americans. The same goes for Major League Baseball in Cleveland, where the Indians are now called the Guardians after succumbing to pressure in July 2021.

Seriously, if Major League Baseball wants to be more inclusive, as they said in announcing the switch, then, I don't know, maybe don't charge so much for food that we need a co-signer to buy a hot pretzel?

It costs the average family of four nearly a thousand dollars to attend a Major League Baseball game. And that's not even counting the grief counseling if they're Mets fans.

Which brings me to my biggest problem with corporate inclusion efforts. The companies lecturing us the most are always the ones with the most exclusionary prices.

Lululemon will bang you $150 for a pair of yoga pants. Sadly, when you're living in a society where 70 percent of Americans are living paycheck to paycheck, shelling out $150 for pants isn't an option for most people, no matter how much better your ass looks in them.

But there's Lululemon, knowing most women in this country would need to sell feet pics to buy their clothes, reminding all of us with a big sign on the front of the store that they "stand for inclusion!"

I always laugh when you're walking through the mall and a business feels the need to put up a huge sign declaring that "in this store we don't tolerate racism, or bigotry, etc." I love how they say it as if there's another store across the way declaring, "We are your Bigotry Headquarters! Come for the low prices; stay to drink from separate water fountains."

All of these corporate gestures are nothing more than straw-man symbolism designed to make you feel good about shopping in their store. Pro sports are doing the same thing by changing logos. But if Cleveland's ownership really wanted to give their fans an emotional boost, they'd spend some cash on better players. The team's payroll is twenty-sixth out of thirty franchises in Major League Baseball. And while money can't buy you love, it can absolutely buy you a pitching staff that just might help you win your first World Series since 1948. That's seventy-five years and counting without a championship! If this drought goes on any longer, the Democrats are gonna start blaming climate change.

Yeah, the good news for Cleveland fans is they no longer have Native American logos on their jerseys. The bad news is when it comes to winning a title, the owners still have reservations.

Neil Young Leads an Attempted Covid Coup on Spotify

In February 2015, a photo of a dress went viral and split the internet in half. The lighting on the image had half the country insisting the dress was blue and black while others furiously fought back that it was white and gold. Then there were the people like me who correctly saw the dress as a waste of fucking time.

The Covid vaccines were a lot like the famous dress in that society had wildly varying opinions, and to this day both sides insist they were right. The only major difference was, in this instance, a choice was forced on our entire country by politicians who took both sides of the issue at differing points in the argument. Okay, and the other difference was if you were wrong, you might die.

Democrats absolutely trashed the vax when President Trump was developing it during the 2020 election season. There were times when political pundits made it sound like Trump was making it himself for his son Barron's school science fair. Even Joe Biden questioned the integrity of the trials during a presidential debate, and Kamala Harris famously went as far as saying, "If Donald Trump tells us to take this shot, I am not taking this shot."

Preach it, girl!

You know, until, of course, you get elected and mandate that everybody take the same shot you were just bashing or lose their jobs.

My problem was not that politicians about-faced on the vaccine; it's that the vaccine didn't work as advertised. And to be super-duper clear, I'm not anti-vax. I'm just anti-bullshit.

I am vaccinated.

Well, at least that's what it says on this card I bought on Craigslist, but the point is we were told from the get-go that we had to get vaccinated because vaccinated people could not get or spread Covid.

To quote the Bible, "That is complete and total horseshit."

(I'm quoting the *Whiskey Bible*. I probably shoulda been more clear.)

Get the vaccine and you're good to go! That was more or less the message of Joe Biden, CDC director Rochelle Walensky, and that little fame whore Dr. Fauci, who took so many different positions on Covid that at this point, more Americans trust Dr. Dre than Dr. Fauci.

Fauci went from no masks to one mask, which ultimately became two masks. And the same guy who was on record multiple times as saying he'd never mandate the vaccine ultimately did exactly that. His justification was that the vaccine would block transmission, so even if you were young and Covid wasn't a threat to your well-being, they were still making you get it anyway because you might otherwise spread it to someone more vulnerable. Logic would tell you that if the vaccine worked to block transmission, there'd be no reason for vaccinated people to care if they were around unvaccinated people. But looking for logic during Covid was like looking for love during spring break. Any method you chose could end with you catching a virus.

They said we had to mask until we had vaccines. Then we had to double mask until we had vaccines. Then we had to mask because the vaccines weren't as good as they hoped. Sometimes it felt like he was flipping a coin; other times it felt like he was trying to cover his ass because of all the coins our National Institutes of Health had given to Chinese labs over the years. It was hard to make heads or tails of it.

But throughout all of this, if you never thought the mask or the vaccines mattered, you spent a lot of time reading about how you could or even should die.

Gone was the left's motto of "My body, my choice," replaced with "Your body, our choice."

A bit of hypocrisy, but again, all of this stuff is baked into the political cake, so I'd be lying if I said it shocked me in any way.

My qualm is that they repeatedly forced these top-down, one-size-fits-all solutions on every one of us. (Yes, I'm aware I might be the first community college student to use the word "qualm," but let's not get sidetracked here.)

They stampeded us with self-righteousness, and to this day nobody has ever acknowledged that they were all the way wrong about everything, including the vaccine stopping transmission. Not only did vaccinated people get and spread Covid in massive numbers, but tens of thousands of vaccinated people died from Covid.

Yet, in the fall of 2021 and the winter of 2022, the vaccine mandate became such a vicious branding battle that celebrities and lawmakers were outright shaming people who didn't want to take it.

Former comedian turned beta male activist Jimmy Kimmel declared on his show that hospitals shouldn't treat unvaccinated people for heart attacks if Covid caused a bed shortage. Arnold Schwarzenegger took time out from shagging his maid to say, "Screw your freedom. You're a schmuck for not wearing a mask." Even Whoopi Goldberg stopped farting on the stagehands at *The View* long enough to say shame, shame, shame on you if you don't get vaccinated.

That last part about Whoopi was a joke. I don't actually know if she's ever stopped farting on the stagehands.

As more high-profile politicians and celebrities began to test positive for Covid, nobody stepped up to own the false advertising of the vaccine. Instead, they tried changing the sale, claiming the whole point of the vax had always been to lessen symptoms. Dozens upon dozens of politicians caught Covid and debased themselves by tweeting the same boilerplate message:

> *I just tested positive for Covid but I'm so thankful I've been vaccinated or this could've been much worse.*

Which is like me saying, *We just found out my wife is pregnant. I just want to express how glad we are to have used a condom or she would've been way more pregnant.*

The point is, whenever lawmakers posted that message, they were demonstrating loyalty in the culture war, but it was doing absolutely nothing to help vaccine enthusiasm.

This wasn't lost on Joe Rogan in February 2022 when he began to question the efficacy of the vax and have on guests to discuss alternative treatments. If you're not familiar, Rogan is the host of the biggest podcast on earth. Yes, it's bigger than mine by a *ton*, but that will change once they start letting my biggest fans use digital devices in prisons. Now, to Joe's credit, he's not getting on the mic and claiming to be an all-knowing authority. He's simply lighting a joint and spitballing with some of the most respected thinkers of our time, and when they're not available, he books Alex Jones.

Everyone listening is welcome to do what they want with the content, because all things considered, the show is a hang. Unlike NPR's *All Things Considered*, which is about as fun as waiting around to be hanged. The Rogan gang does get into heavy stuff at times, but the idea that a guy jacked up on TRT, HGH, and POT would be subjected to a higher level of scrutiny than the public health officials who lied to us seems a little silly.

That's exactly what happened when Rogan announced he'd gotten Covid and pursued other treatments. The outrage mob said he had blood on his hands for not pushing the vax, and they also falsely claimed he was pushing medicine on humans that was meant for horses.

This was the actual line of attack that got Neil Young to spring into action: gullible goobers were taking horse paste because right-wing extremist Joe Rogan told them it treats Covid.

Now, Joe Rogan is a guy who voted for Bernie Sanders when he first came on the scene. Last I checked, Bernie wasn't the most right-wing candidate in the world, although he has gotten richer preaching his anti-capitalist manifesto than most right-wing capitalists could ever dream.

The bigger issue is that the discoverers of the drug Rogan mentioned, Ivermectin, won a Nobel Peace Prize in 2015 for its treatment of river blindness in humans. Many developing world studies showed it improved outcomes in Covid as well. But online there was more interest in ruining people for disagreeing than having an actual discussion.

This is yet another area where the incentivized conflict of social media is really hurting society: we're now fighting each other more than our common enemies. Covid-19 attacked all of us the same, whether you're a Republican or a Democrat. The only exception being if you were out rioting in the summer of 2020, in which case public health officials actually said you were okay to be there while the rest of the country was barred from going to work, school, or church.

Most objective observers realized that granting a protest exemption to social distancing guidelines was political science and not laboratory science, but anyone who voiced an objection caught the same vicious blowback Rogan did.

Therein lies the other problem with the mob mentality enveloping social media. They become so omnipotent that they make people a "prisoner of the moment." The trending wisdom of a particular news cycle is now being shot at us out of a fire hose with so much force and fury that it completely overwhelms our ability to think beyond the blast.

It's moments like this that bait otherwise smart people into making stupid decisions, sometimes to gain currency from like-minded mob members, other times because their emotions genuinely inform them to believe stupid things.

Neil Young seemingly did both when he announced in January 2021 that he was pulling all of his music off Spotify in hopes it would lead them to cut ties with Joe Rogan.

Not only was this dumb by scientific standards, but it was a total abandonment of everything that fueled Young's rise to superstardom.

There is no bigger creative about-face than singing "Rockin' in the Free World" and then telling people to shut up and do what the government tells them to. Young pulled his music off Spotify and urged other artists to do the same and stop supporting Spotify's deadly misinformation about Covid.

Hey hey, my my / Censorship *can never die . . .*

What a sellout!

Let me give you more of Neil's grandstanding ridiculousness to add some additional perspective:

"Spotify represents 60% of the streaming of my music to listeners around the world. . . . Yet my [record label] stood with me, recognizing the threat the COVID misinformation on SPOTIFY posed to the world—particularly for our young people who think everything they hear on SPOTIFY is true," Young declared on his website. "Unfortunately it is not."

To be clear, the biggest piece of Covid misinformation fed to the American people came from the folks who told us this was a pandemic of the unvaccinated, as if they were the only ones who could get Covid.

The biggest culprits in cavalierly pushing things on young people were not Spotify podcasters but government officials like Gavin Newsom who pushed vaccinations for children despite the fact that every other major industrialized nation was refraining from doing so.

History will show that nothing our government did with Covid worked. Studies have not shown that mask mandates worked, nor that closures worked, nor that vaccines stopped transmission. Neil Young's attempt to get Joe Rogan kicked off Spotify didn't work either. It did get some of his other contemporaries, like the great Joni Mitchell, to pull their music, which had to be challenging to explain because a lot of her fans thought Spotify was a hand cream.

I can tell that joke because nobody reading this book is worse with technology than me. Like, I once asked an Amish guy for help with my iPad.

As for Rogan, he's still out there smoking weed, questioning science, and reaching more people in a day than most podcasters will reach in a lifetime, even with a vaccine and all fifty-six boosters.

This is a win for all of us because Americans have every right to question our government's motives, especially when it involves our health and a massive shift on a vaccine mandate that they turned out to be wrong about.

Which is to say that when Neil was younger, he was right to speak out against overzealous government as he did in songs like "Ohio." But the rage-driven hive mind of social media convinced the Old Man version of Neil Young to look past the Needle and the Damage Done to the credibility of government health institutions that repeatedly failed us.

I don't doubt that he wanted to help, that he has a Heart of Gold, if you will. But let the record show that Joe was right and Neil was wrong, For What It's Worth.

Okay, pal.

I'll stop the Neil Young puns before someone drowns me Down by the River. The moral of the story is that joining the outrage mob is often a fool's errand, so Teach Your Children Well.

Office Christmas Parties

Let's start here. Everybody knows a guy or a gal who gets a little too frisky at the office holiday party. And if you don't, it's because it's *you*.

Armed with this drunken data in the fall of 2018, thousands of companies decided to cancel their annual parties in the wake of the #MeToo movement for fear that somebody might flirt their way into a lawsuit.

Let's face it, nobody wants to wake up hungover after a night of Christmas karaoke and do *anything*, let alone give a legal deposition, because Bob in Accounting asked Jackie in Tech Support if she wanted to see Frosty the Snowman's North Pole.

Although these days Bob would probably get in more trouble for not using the DEI-approved description: Snow-*person*.

But the point is the point.

Many corporations benched their bartenders after #MeToo because the potential for legal peril was everywhere. Holiday office parties have a storied history of drunken debauchery that's loaded with off-color comments and all kinds of coworker hookups.

And if you don't think coworkers hook up after office parties, you've never driven a taxi in New York City. Trust me: I have seen some things in my back seat over the years that *no one* should see.

Let's just say there's a lot of mistletoe in the Land of Misfit Toys. I'll spare you the specifics on the nudity, but Taxi Santa has delivered some very suspicious packages over the years. Part of me wonders if companies really canceled parties because they were just looking out for cabbies who've been exposed to all this traumatic holiday horniness? Believe me, nothing you'll ever do in life prepares you for the moment you pick up two tiny elves outside the Macy's in Herald Square, only to watch them tear off their costumes and stuff each other's stockings in the back seat. It happened to me after a Macy's party in 2009, and my world has never been the same.

Making matters worse, I can't even call someone a "tiny elf" in this day and age because I work at Fox News, where HR makes us say "Gutfeld-American."

Regardless, with #MeToo mayhem running up legal bills everywhere, nearly half of all companies canceled office parties in 2018. Of the ones who went through with them, just 48 percent served alcohol.

In lieu of an annual booze-a-thon, some companies opted for team-building activities, such as a visit to an "Escape the Room" game. For my money, this is worse than getting hit on by someone you don't like. After all, isn't trapping people in a tiny room that they can't get out of until they solve pointless puzzles what companies do the rest of the year?

This trend of playing "Escape the Room" gained even more steam during the pandemic, as group hangouts weren't even an option. Yes, a lot of companies have come back to the holiday party in a post-Covid world, but as of this writing, 30 percent of companies are still skipping it altogether. I completely understand why the "People Team" wants to play a little defense, but as a guy who's made his living saying crazy things, I feel for folks being denied that one day a year to drop their conversational guard a little bit.

The problem is, you can't really take this position without sounding like the handsy guy who brings his own mistletoe to the party, but let the record show that's absolutely not my deal.

For one, I'm somehow married to a next-level babe. You've gotta see it to believe it.

But, two, even if I was single, hello?

I am a former taxi driver who's somehow working in television. Everyone I come into contact with is cartoonishly out of my league. Most of the guys you see next to me look like they belong on TV. I look like the guy who installed your TV.

It's a gift that makes me more relatable to viewers, but, trust me, it's a curse if you wanna hit on chicks who hang out at the White House and you hang out in the Waffle House. I think most husbands who've seen me on TV are more worried I'm going to steal their wife's clothes than her heart.

My pro–office party argument is that America has gotten so PC that everyone is being forced to walk around with a law firm in their head that screens their words twenty-four hours a day. Just because that's a better premise than every Pixar movie doesn't mean we should do it. It's an exhausting way to live, and it's the entire thesis of this book: we need to stop appeasing the censorship brigades because they keep narrowing the lanes in which we can enjoy ourselves.

If anything, #MeToo should allow us to feel safer, knowing that any boss who tries to pressure an intern into going home with him is definitely waking up next to a pink slip in the morning. Just not the kind he'd hoped for.

There's a cathartic value in getting your team together for drinks, ripping on each other, flirting, and just generally behaving in ways you don't on every other day of the year.

The reason comedy clubs are experiencing such a boom right now is that people need to escape the corporatization of life to a place where they can hear things that wouldn't otherwise fly in the office.

Again, I am not saying the whole purpose of an office party is to tell crass jokes and try to score with your coworkers (although I would have definitely said this in my twenties). What I am saying is you'd rather have a team of people who can tell a joke and take a joke than a bunch of uptight hall monitors who write down every off-color comment because they've been trained to seek out grievances.

Who wants to live like that?

The truth is, at our core, nobody does, because it's miserable.

Which is why, for my money, every company needs to bring back the bartenders next holiday season. Sure, it could lead to a couple of silly statements, but if you do the party right, you won't remember any of them the next day anyway.

President Trump

The best summary of Donald Trump's four years in the White House came on his very first day, when our forty-third president, George W. Bush, was caught on a hot mic at the end of Trump's inaugural address saying, "That was some weird shit."

Four years, two impeachments, one pandemic, and a bazillion Twitter rants later, President Bush looked prophetic in his characterization. I'm not sure if W. discovered a time machine, but he still hasn't found weapons of mass destruction in Iraq.

Too soon?

For my money, 43 will always be a total badass for throwing out the greatest first pitch in baseball history before game three of the 2001 World Series. I was in Yankee Stadium that night, sitting in a right-field seat that was much, *much* farther up than the ticket broker claimed it would be. Apparently, when the cigar-chomping guy in the chauffeur hat took my cash and promised me, "These seats have an amazing view," he forgot to add, "of Jupiter." It's not every day you get to eat a Milky Way while sitting in the Milky Way, but there I was, in the very last row, at the tippy top of the upper deck.

That said, nothing was higher than the tension in New York City when Bush landed that night. The country had just been hit by the biggest terror attack in its history. Widespread paranoia about gathering in large groups had swept the nation, and for the first time for many of us we were going through metal detectors to enter the stadium.

As hard as it is to imagine in a world where we now sell our biometric data just to get us through security faster, there was a time when we used to walk straight into sports stadiums without going through a single metal detector or X-ray machine. We didn't even have TSA pat-downs at most airports back then, which is a shame, because I've enjoyed quite a few of them over the years.

All of this enhanced security was new at the stadium when Marine One touched down in the Bronx, and everyone was understandably a little freaked out by it all. But with the rubble still smoldering a few miles south at Ground Zero, Bush courageously strode to the mound in the center of a wide-open stadium and gave a big, confident wave that made 57,000 nervous Yankees fans feel a little more like their usual bloodthirsty selves. From there, despite wearing a bulletproof vest, he threw a perfect strike that absolutely tore the roof off the place.

I was completely blown away by the symbolic power of the presidency to rally a wayward nation with a single act, but that's exactly what he did. With one sixty-foot toss of a baseball, Bush gave a country its confidence back. I don't mean to sound like we just got high in a Volkswagen bus but, seriously, "it was *deep*, man." When that pitch hit the catcher's mitt, the crowd let out a roar that throttled my beer-filled body. Although, to be fair, some of that shaking might have been caused by the asteroid belt passing through in the section below mine.

As I look back on all of this now, it doesn't surprise me that Bush thought Trump's inauguration was a little weird, given how far off the rails the 2016 race had been compared to previous campaigns, including his own.

Presidential elections normally have a buttoned-up country-club vibe. At least, they did until Donald Trump went full *Caddyshack* and reprised the role of Rodney Dangerfield barreling into the clubhouse and insulting everyone in sight. There was even a pudgy gopher, thanks to Brian Stelter.

Someday we'll see late-night TV infomercials selling a collection of Trump's campaign events as if they were Dean Martin roasts. Picture the voice-over as you see him onstage trashing journalists, war heroes, debate moderators, you name it:

All the insults are here! From Crooked Hillary to Little Marco! The Fake News may be lying, but we're telling the truth when we say you've gotta order Donald Trump's greatest insults, so pick up the phone now!

Trump ran for president of the United States the way most people run for president of their fantasy football league. He roasted everyone on the group chat mercilessly. And to top it all off, he won the big prize just weeks after the *Access Hollywood* tape surfaced. He famously shrugged that one off as "locker room talk," but I've gotta be honest, I've been in a *ton* of locker rooms and I've never heard of this technique before. Luckily for him, anything sounded better than grabbing a voting lever and pulling it for Hillary, so in the end, like Bush, Trump went home with a W.

Even so, we were all a little thrown by the sight of Trump taking the oath of office on January 20, 2017. Especially when you consider that, up until then, we'd seen hundreds of people lose their jobs for tweeting off-color things. Yet there we were, watching a guy accept the highest job in the land after breaking every social media rule there was.

Compare that to Joe Biden, who can't be writing any of his own tweets, because if someone typed the way he speaks it would look like a cat walked across a keyboard. There's also the small fact that Biden gets lost so often when he's leaving the stage that he'll go down in history as the only president who takes more time to exit a speech than he does to give one. Nobody wants that guy running a Twitter account.

As for Trump, the man who rose to presidential prominence on Twitter ultimately left 1600 Pennsylvania Avenue with no account access to speak of after the company banned him for violating something called its "Glorification of Violence" policy in the aftermath of the January 6 attack on the Capitol.

Here's the official statement announcing the ban:

On January 8, 2021, President Donald J. Trump Tweeted:

The 75,000,000 great American Patriots who voted for me, AMERICA FIRST, and MAKE AMERICA GREAT AGAIN, will have a GIANT VOICE long into the future. They will not be disrespected or treated unfairly in any way, shape or form!!!

Shortly thereafter, the President Tweeted:

To all of those who have asked, I will not be going to the Inauguration on January 20th.

Due to the ongoing tensions in the United States, and an uptick in the global conversation in regards to the people who violently stormed the Capitol on January 6, 2021, these two Tweets must be read in the context of broader events in the country and the ways in which the President's statements can be mobilized by different audiences, including to incite violence, as well as in the context of the pattern of behavior from this account in recent weeks. After assessing the language in these Tweets against our Glorification of Violence policy, we have determined that these Tweets are in violation of the Glorification of Violence Policy and the user @realDonaldTrump should be immediately permanently suspended from the service. *[emphasis added]*

So, to translate that into English, Twitter claimed it was banning Trump because he was questioning the legitimacy of the election and it had to protect our democracy. To be clear, the company never banned any of the Democrats who told us Trump and Russia stole the 2016 election, but the company justified what looked like a double standard by citing the potential for Trump's tweets to cause more violence like we saw at the Capitol on January 6.

But even the concerns about violence felt like a reach on their part, because in the summer of 2020, as we were watching the George Floyd riots cause billions of dollars in damages and claim dozens of lives, Twitter wasn't banning any of the politicians who cheered them on. Kamala Harris tweeted a link encouraging people to bail out protesters in Minneapolis after the town saw over one hundred businesses burned down and a police station torched to boot. Yet there was no ban when she and her fellow Democrats seemingly condoned that carnage, which only led to more of it over the coming weeks.

The truth is there has always been a different standard for reacting to Donald Trump whether we're talking about election claims or his handling of classified documents, which he was indicted for in June 2023.

Other people had done it, namely Hillary Clinton and Joe Biden, but Trump was the only one charged. At the time, we were told that Joe and Hillary avoided charges because they were more cooperative with their investigations, but in the end the law is still the law, no?

If I commit a murder, the cops aren't going to let me go because I was more cooperative with my investigation than other murderers. Trust me, I'm married seventeen years. I've looked into it on more than one occasion. But the never-ending shifting of standards in an effort to get Trump is one of the main driving points for why he and his supporters didn't trust the outcome of the 2020 election.

During his four years in office, the Democrats had proven repeatedly that they would try anything they could think of to stop this dude. From the Russian collusion narrative to the impeachment for wrongdoing in Ukraine, there wasn't a day of Trump's presidency when the Democrats and their allies in the media weren't assuring us that the sky was falling. And like all doomsday preachers, they collected plenty of money from their gullible flock through the higher ratings they got while he was in office.

All of that changed when he exited the spotlight after the Twitter ban. Many on the left rejoiced at the time, thinking this was a *yuge* victory, but the truth is everybody lost when Trump got muted.

Here's the deal. Our speech rights are enshrined in the United States Constitution, and for good reason. When we outsource them to places like Silicon Valley, we run the risk that any of us can be silenced in the public square for defying the political views of whoever's running the popular app of the day.

This is exactly what happened when Twitter banned doctors from tweeting various arguments about Covid that contradicted the preferred political narrative. Non-doctors got to decide what was an acceptable medical idea to discuss. Which is like letting vegans determine the menu at a steak house. You're probably not going to stay in business for long, although the Yelp reviews would be pretty hilarious.

The point is you don't have to like *anything* Trump's ever tweeted to know that if big tech oligarchs become the gatekeepers of speech, so much so that they can mute a *president*, we're all in danger of being silenced down the road, which is *no bueno*. (Sorry to speak French at such a crucial moment, but sometimes I like to show off what I learned in community college.)

Freedom of speech is the most important right any of us has, which is why it's in the very First Amendment in the Constitution. For that reason, nobody should support any limits to our speech because again, and again, and again: When they control the language, they control *the people*.

Take it from a child of the '80s. "Control" is a great song by Janet Jackson. But it's a terrible thing to give anyone over our ability to question the government, even if they are doing so as an outgoing president.

That being said, when Trump's Twitter ban was announced, everybody on the left was quick to remind the "free enterprise Republicans" that a private company can do whatever it wants. Which, of course, backfired on them spectacularly two years later when Twitter exercised its aforementioned rights to sell the platform to Elon Musk. Gone was all that liberal talk of private companies doing whatever they want, replaced with "We're all gonna die!" And the funniest part about Elon Musk buying Twitter is that just about everybody freaking out the loudest was driving a Tesla.

You'd never know from consuming any mainstream media source now, but Elon Musk used to be the patron saint of green-energy liberalism. Not only was he the biggest electric car manufacturer in the world, but his SpaceX company was using its Starlink satellites to provide internet access in parts of the world that didn't traditionally have it. The left loved this guy, shoveling billions in subsidies his way, right up until he put his money behind free speech for everyone, at which point they immediately recast him as a billionaire white supremacist supervillain. It's the same transactional nature they displayed toward Donald Trump when he made the transition from celebrity loudmouth to political loudmouth.

It's almost impossible to quantify just how massive the left's about-face was on Trump when he threw his red hat in the ring in 2016. Yes, he made his entrance in some pretty off-color terms, but this was the standard public persona of a guy who was an absolute constant in the public eye for decades as he hobnobbed with every member of polite society, including the Clintons and just about every other prominent politician in America. Trump had a TV show on NBC for fifteen seasons. He appeared regularly on shows like *Howard Stern* and *Oprah*. He was tight with Barbara Walters and was a regular on *The View* before it became the highest-rated show in Guantánamo Bay. Yeah, you can't waterboard terrorists anymore but you don't need to when you can threaten them with a hot take from Sunny Hostin.

I kid, but I'm serious when I say Trump was accepted by everyone and had been a fixture on late-night shows since the 1980s. Yet when he came down the escalator in the golden age of outrage, a lot of the same folks who appeared on *Celebrity Apprentice* and showed up to all of his parties now felt pressured to play along with the pretend narrative that Trump was a love child between Darth Vader and a spray-tanned Hitler. Hell, Jimmy Fallon almost got chased off the *Tonight Show* when he mussed Trump's hair in a September 2016 interview because the mob said he was "normalizing Trump." Yet Trump had just hosted *Saturday Night Live* on the same channel the previous year and nobody said a word because he was already normalized.

What changed? Not Trump.

His character was always that of a crass, pugnacious asshole who talked a ton of shit to everyone. A billionaire playboy, known for a weapons-grade ego, who was given to bombast on a comical level. The only thing different when he entered politics was the reaction to his over-the-top demeanor. Suddenly the same liberal politicians who took his donations now slammed him for being rich. And many Republicans like Mitt Romney who craved his endorsements when they were running suddenly said he was a danger to the country. Of course, that didn't stop Mitt from interviewing for a cabinet position after Trump won, but we shouldn't be surprised by the shameless desperation of a guy who wears mom jeans.

I'm not writing this to defend Trump, because at this point there's too much to defend him against. And while he obviously contributes to a lot of his problems, it was the manufactured hysteria toward his entrance into politics that's allowed the left to justify taking so many unprecedented lines of attack against the guy.

Think about it. We had never indicted a president *once* in the first 246 years of our nation's history. Yet, at the rate we're going now, it's only a matter of time before Democrats charge Trump with child neglect for failing to help Kevin McCallister in *Home Alone 2*.

Listen, I'm never going to be the guy who tells you people shouldn't be charged if they break the law. But the last thing anyone should be trying to take away is speech rights, especially Trump's. Yes, the guy throws a lot of wild pitches. No, he shouldn't be silenced, because if it happens to him, it'll eventually happen to us.

To his credit, Elon Musk recognized the threat posed by all of this weaponized censorship and reinstated Trump's Twitter account shortly after buying the app for 44 billion bucks in November 2022. The doomsday prophets on the left predicted we'd all be dead in the streets within twenty-four hours of Trump's reinstatement, but history will note that the sky refused to fall yet again. Must be all that climate change.

Trump didn't run right back to Twitter, choosing instead to stay on the social media app he owned, Truth Social. I don't have an account there, but from what I've read of his posts, there seems to be a technical glitch that only allows him to write in ALL CAPS.

Sad!

It's unclear if he'll ever make Twitter an everyday thing again, but even if Trump decides it's completely off the table, I can't say I'd blame him. Like most of social media, Twitter is nothing more than a Fight Club for people who don't wanna get hit. No matter what hour of the day you tweet, some misfit toy will be standing by to argue with you about *whatever* you post. Share a picture of your dog and wish him a happy birthday. Within seconds, a broken person will remind you that they won't be serving birthday cake in the prison where your preferred political leader is headed.

It's disturbing, but it's also reality, because Twitter runs on incentivized conflict. The people who show up there to score digital dopamine have been taught that the quickest way to "fix" is to put down folks they disagree with in the harshest terms allowable by law. When you realize this, it's no wonder so many people have lost their jobs over the years for tweeting reckless things. However, it's some wonder that only *one guy* in history got a job by tweeting like he got paid by the put-down, and that job was *president of the United States*.

In the end, not even he was safe. And while Trump didn't lose his job because of Twitter, he did lose Twitter because of the way he lost his job. Sure, he's since been welcomed back, but he's probably better off staying away, because *nowhere in the world* is there a guy who'd be better off if only he spent more time on Twitter.

If you disagree, you can take it up with me @JimmyFailla.

Canceled

We regret to inform you that this chapter has been canceled due to sensitivities associated with the letter **Q**. Many Americans are rightfully concerned about the **Q**Anon conspiracy theory, and thousands of our British readers are still coping with the **Q**ueen of England's death.

We'd also like to distance ourselves from the 1980s arcade classic **Q***bert, which took place in an intolerant time when there were only two genders and one joystick.

Looking back now, we realize one of the biggest games of that era wasn't about Pac-Man or Ms. Pac-Man; it was about transphobia.

We promise to educate ourselves and strive to do better with the remaining chapters in this book. If it's any consolation to those of you hoping to read the **Q** chapter, please know it might be the weakest letter in the alphabet.

Not only does **Q** need the letter **U** to support it in 99.9 percent of the words it appears in, but in some instances **Q** is not even cool enough to play itself on a roadside gas station sign.

If you don't believe me, you've never shopped at a *Kwik* Mart.

Roseanne

I've always considered Roseanne Barr to be my generation's Joan Rivers because she rose to stand-up superstardom at a time when it was very much a man's game. Anyone who tells jokes for a living knows it's high praise to compare someone to Joan Rivers. After all, if there was a comedy Mount Rushmore, Joan's face would definitely be on it.

We'd just have to figure out *which* face.

Relax, we can tell plastic surgery jokes about the dead. Especially a woman who joked when she was alive that "I've had so much plastic surgery, when I die they're gonna donate my body to Tupperware." If you're wondering, my favorite Joan Rivers joke was "My vagina is like Newark. Men know it exists, but they don't want to visit."

If only the world felt the same way about Twitter.

Thankfully for Joan's sake, Twitter didn't exist when she was taking over the comedy world, because she told tons of hysterical jokes about race, religion, and sex that might've rubbed the outrage mob the wrong way. Now, technically speaking, Twitter didn't exist when Roseanne was taking over either. But it did exist when she was taking pills and sharing her thoughts on politics thirty years later. History will show that pills/Twitter might be the world's most disastrous combination outside of Biden/Harris.

In May 2018, just two months into a revival of her self-titled sitcom, the woman who rose to fame as a "domestic goddess" was at home, doing what she called "Ambien tweeting," when she dropped a joke that caused ABC to drop her show the next morning.

The tweet in question was about former Obama White House advisor Valerie Jarrett, whom Barr described as being the result if *muslim brotherhood & planet of the apes had a baby.*

As you've probably figured out by now, I'm not the biggest fan of censoring speech. But, speaking as your friend, I can tell you there's never going to be a scenario in life that will work out to your benefit if you compare a woman to a primate.

This was a wild pitch, even by the sewer-like standards of Twitter. Barr seemed to know it, so she deleted the tweet a few hours later. By then, the showbiz world had caught wind of it, and the smoke was rising quickly. And this time it wasn't from Ro Ro's bong.

Her costar on the show, Sara Gilbert, tweeted multiple condemnations in the hours following the tweet, distancing herself and the crew as far from Roseanne's take as possible. Comedian and contributing producer Wanda Sykes tweeted that she was quitting the show outright. Barr was also attacked by other famous comedians, including Al Sharpton.

She issued several apologies, saying she was under the influence of pills and claiming she thought Valerie Jarrett was white. The network executives weren't buying any of it, not even the pill story. Which is surprising, because if anyone is out there buying pills, it's Hollywood executives.

Less than twelve hours after she hit send, the president of ABC Entertainment Group, Channing Dungey, announced her firing, saying in a tweet:

> *Roseanne's Twitter Statement is abhorrent, repugnant, and inconsistent with our values, and we have decided to cancel her show. There was only one thing to do here, and that was the right thing.*

It will go down as one of the fastest cancels in history, with the punishment being doled out before most Americans had even heard about the crime.

Now, I'm not here to defend Roseanne's comments, because I need my job. And it goes without saying that her statement was insanely stupid. Even if she truly thought Valerie Jarrett was white, you're not exactly killing the lady with kindness by saying she was born when a bunch of terrorrist dudes shagged some horny apes. Nor are you being historically accurate, because if you know anything about the Muslim Brotherhood, those fellas are more attracted to goats.

What I can tell you is that while Twitter lost its mind, most comics weren't surprised by Roseanne's statement because she's a shock jock who made a career out of offending people.

We didn't agree with it. But we also didn't get out of bed that day thinking she was Mother Teresa, because from the second Roseanne hit the comedy scene, her credo was always *Find the line and cross it.* It stood out because most comics in the 1980s lived by the credo *Find the line and snort it.*

R.I.P. Sam Kinison. You were the fucking man.

Roseanne once upset the whole country by singing an embarrassingly off-key rendition of the national anthem before a San Diego

Padres game in 1990. How she avoided a fine for noise pollution is beyond me, but she doubled down on her bad performance by grabbing her crotch and spitting, which made it exponentially more crass. Everyone was pissed about it, including former president George H. W. Bush, who labeled her performance "disgraceful." Although, to be fair, he could have said that about any Padres game that year.

She caught holy hell in 2009 for dressing like Adolf Hitler in a photo shoot for a satirical Jewish magazine called *Heeb*. It's worth noting that she's Jewish herself, and she was mocking Hitler and not his victims. But let the record show that you should never dress like a Nazi. Talking to you, Prince Harry.

Roseanne survived those controversies because social media wasn't a thing yet, and you couldn't mobilize a cancel posse as quickly as you can today. Hard as it might be to imagine now, there was a time in this country when people would do horrifically stupid things all the time and it would just blow over. Because, at the end of the day, we all knew the difference between a tasteless joke and a terror attack, and so did the people in charge.

If you don't believe me, ask Joy Behar, Howard Stern, Jimmy Kimmel, and Jimmy Fallon, all of whom wore blackface in various sketches and didn't even get a slap on the wrist. No, the only people who were punished for Joy Behar's jokes were the audience.

The truth is this one would've blown over too. Yes, there would've been seventy-two hours of rage tweets and horrible hashtags for ABC, but most fans would've stuck around because Roseanne was just doing what she's always done, which is saying offensive things. The members of the speech police were never going to watch a show like this anyway, so in the end ABC canceled *Roseanne* to appease the people who weren't tuning in.

If the network had stood its ground, the fans of Roseanne's ridiculousness would not have bailed and given a win to all the self-righteous hall monitors they loathe. And once that was established, the mob would've done what they always do when people refuse to back down, which is nothing. If you don't believe me, ask Dave Chappelle. The cancel crowd has tried a million times to make him bend the knee, but he's always extended his middle finger instead, and there was nothing they could do. Sure, Netflix let them march outside its headquarters for a few days, but they were only doing that because most of those protesters looked like they could use the exercise.

The mob accumulates power by convincing the world that jokes need to be vigilantly policed, because if you make fun of something, people are more likely to violently attack it. But if that were the case, every member of Nickelback would be dead by now because the entire world has been making fun of that band for decades.

Sometimes the mob's social pressure stampede terrifies a company like ABC into acting, but it's a bad formula for all of us in the long run because treating speech as violence is creating a backward world where there's a lot more focus on what you say than on what you do.

Chris Brown literally assaulted Rihanna after the 2009 Grammys and was back onstage winning more Grammys within two years. Yet Kanye West remains banned for saying some insanely stupid shit on Twitter. I'm not defending Kanye's take. Heavens no. All I'm saying is that outrage culture has created a world where you're better off attacking someone physically than verbally. This will never square with the former cabdriver in me. I'm telling you, no matter how many times a driver gets punched or kicked while someone's running out on the fare, you never once say to yourself, *Thank gosh they didn't call me names instead.* Although I should admit that to this day, when I pay to get beat up on Craigslist, I do ask them to throw in a couple of disparaging terms.

As it stands, Roseanne came all the way back to have one of the most talked-about stand-up specials of 2023. Canceling her didn't change society in any meaningful way, and none of the people who pushed for her firing had much to say about her return. Proving that, as always, the cause was never as important as the control.

I got a chance to interview Roseanne when she was making the promotional rounds—because, naturally, when you're trying to push a stand-up special, you go to the *biggest* radio show around. (And once you get done with Brian Kilmeade's show, you come do mine, because it's right next door.)

I was thrilled for a chance to assess her character face-to-face, because the one true superpower that most cabdrivers have, aside from their ability to go weeks without showering, is that all cabbies are excellent judges of character. We have to be, because when you make a living picking up strangers in the middle of the night, you need to spot the difference between a guy who wants to head home and a guy who wants to put your head in the trunk. Don't get me wrong, there are plenty of maddening shifts where you're *hoping* someone will kill you, but for the most part you do try to survive.

Having had the chance to run Roseanne through my taxi sensor, I can tell you she didn't seem remotely close to a hateful person. She's definitely fed up with a lot of things in society, and she is well past the point of having any conversational filter whatsoever—mainly because she never had one to begin with. This is a woman who burst onto the scene in the 1980s precisely because she had zero fucks to give, and the country found it refreshing.

She was syrupy sweet to me off the air, and she didn't have to be, because this was before I became famous enough to get recognized by the manager at a Chinese buffet. Granted, it was because the last time I was there I got caught trying to take home crab legs, but the point is, my star is rising. At least, that's what it said in the fortune cookie.

Was her tweet about Valerie Jarrett awful? Yes. Does that make her a Klansman? No. She's a potty-mouthed, cranky comic who got carried away on Twitter, where fighting over politics brings out the absolute worst in everyone. Remember that old-school anti-drug commercial where they show butter sizzling in a frying pan and the voice-over says, "This is drugs," then someone cracks open an egg in it, and as it fries, the voice-over says, "This is your *brain* on drugs"? They could absolutely make that same commercial to show how social media warps your judgment:

"This is Twitter. This is your *brain* on Twitter."

And then a protest would break out because they didn't use cage-free eggs.

Here's the deal. Roseanne has been a public figure for about thirty-five years and we've never found her threatening before. We know who she is. She was the same person when ABC hired her as when ABC fired her. And while it makes perfect sense if another company doesn't want to work with her going forward because of things we've known about for decades, it was still all the way stupid to fire her over one terrible tweet. She's always said dumb things, but that doesn't mean any of us should be okay with the idea of people losing their jobs for it.

Unlike Roseanne, the rest of us aren't sitting on sitcom money if the mob puts out a hit on our careers. For that reason alone, we need to bring back the idea of forgiveness in the court of public opinion.

I'm not just saying that because Roseanne is a conservative. The same grace should be extended toward every huge liberal who's ever told a tasteless racial joke, like Howard Stern or Jimmy Kimmel or even Joy Behar. Seriously. Every one of you should know that if I ever wind up driving a taxi again, I'd still be willing to pick you up no matter what direction you're trending in on Twitter.

Don't take that offer lightly, because the way this book is going, there's a pretty good chance it'll happen.

The Slap

Will Smith smacking Chris Rock at the Oscars is the most famous moment in the history of the ceremony. I know a lot of people take issue with the Fresh Prince for leaving some "Fresh Prints" on Chris's face, and rightfully so. But in Will's defense, he is the first person to get liberals to acknowledge Black-on-Black crime.

He's also proof that these days everybody really does get a trophy, even if they just assaulted someone in front of millions of viewers around the world.

Technically speaking, Will's actions could have led to an extra trophy being given out for "Best Supporting Witness."

We don't know if the Academy considered my new category, but we do know that moments after he'd stormed the stage at the Dolby Theatre, Smith returned to the scene of the crime to accept the Best Actor award. There weren't as many right hooks as on his first trip onstage, but the entire audience was staring in disbelief nonetheless. Now, to be fair, most of the raised eyebrows in the crowd were from plastic surgery. Even so, it has to be the most surreal moment in awards show history.

We begin with a bit of background on how and why this whole hullaballoo happened:

Jada Pinkett Smith suffers from a medical condition known as alopecia, which causes hair loss. We know this because she'd previously opened up about it on her *Red Table Talk* podcast. I'm not sure Chris Rock knew that when he made a reference to her look, but what he and everyone else in the room absolutely *did* know was that Jada also told her podcast listeners that she'd slept with men during her marriage who weren't her husband, including R&B singer August Alsina, who was over twenty years younger than Will.

Incredibly, Will Smith was *co-hosting* the 2018 episode in which she'd made the confession, and the whole thing was so bonkers that 31 million watched it the first day alone. There's an old saying about marriage: "You don't do your laundry in public." Apparently, Jada had never heard it, or the other saying about not doing your sidepieces in public.

Hearing her discuss the men she'd been sleeping with in front of her Hollywood megastar of a husband left the world with so many questions. Mainly, how is Will cool with this? And can I get her number?

So let the record show that in this recipe for disaster, the first ingredient was a cuckolded husband with an ego the size of the Hollywood sign. Complicating matters further, Rock also had a history of mocking Jada at the Oscars.

During his show-opening monologue in 2016, Rock made a reference to the fact that she was among a group of lesser-known actors who were vowing to boycott that year's ceremony:

Jada boycotting the Oscars is like me boycotting Rihanna's panties. I wasn't invited.

So understand it's not the first time he's joked about Jada, but this time around she happened to be sitting next to her emasculated husband, whom everyone in the room knows she'd cheated on. You'd think it would have to hurt Will Smith's pride on some level. If there was any doubt, it all went out the window at 9:30 p.m. on Sunday, March 27, 2022:

Rock had just taken the stage to present the award for Best Documentary Feature Film.

This is essentially the last award before the true stretch run of the show, where the categories that make the most headlines are decided. I'm talking Best Director, Best Actor, and Best Picture.

That's not to say the Best Documentary Feature Film category doesn't matter. But it's usually when most of the male actors have left the room for a bump of cocaine, and many females have gone to the bathroom to puke one last time so they can look extra skinny in the after-party photos.

"There's *no* business . . . like *show* business!"

The point I'm trying to make is normally Best Documentary Feature Film is a forgettable moment.

Not tonight.

Rock came onstage all smiling and happy-faced like he always does. I know he starred in a sitcom called *Everybody Hates Chris*, but he has a vibe that makes every room happier when he enters, especially the strippers. This dude knows his way around a champagne room, and he's as good a comic as there is.

He opened by addressing the post-pandemic reality, saying, "Wow, what a night. Nobody is wearing a mask. Everybody here is breathing raw dog tonight."

A big laugh from the crowd spilled into his shout-out to Denzel Washington.

"Denzel! Macbeth? Loved it! I love the part where he said, 'King Lear got nothing on me'!"

Rock was doing an impression of King Lear, quoting Denzel's character in *Training Day*. The room exploded in laughter.

His jokes were two for two, and the crowd was eating it up.

Still on script, he surfed a wave of laughter into his third joke about the fact that Javier Bardem and his wife, Penelope Cruz, are both being nominated for Best Actor awards.

"You know who's got the hardest job here tonight? Javier Bardem and his wife are both nominated. Now if she loses, *he can't win*! He is praying Will Smith wins, like, *Please, Lord*."

Three for three.

Everyone in the room breaks up at this one, including Will Smith, who was shown on camera laughing as his hands rested on his knees, where they didn't stay long.

Before Rock's eyes could return to the teleprompter, he noticed the Smiths in the front row. At this point he went off script and made a reference to her shaved head, saying, "Jada, I love you. *G.I. Jane 2*, can't wait to see it. All right?"

Four for four.

The entire audience is seen laughing, including Will Smith.

Jada, on the other hand, rolled her eyes in a pronounced state of disgust. A face like this one would normally wind up in every meme for the next six months if it weren't for what her husband did next.

The room was rolling in laughter, but Rock could see her visible disdain for the joke, so he attempted to address it, smiling sheepishly at their table and saying:

"It's—that was a—that was a nice one! Okay, I'm out here—"

At which point Rock sees Smith striding toward him onstage and jokingly says, "Uh-oh—Richard!"

It was a reference to the character Will Smith portrayed in *King Richard*.

By the time the words came out of Rock's mouth, the Raging Royal had clocked him with a vicious right-handed slap that swung downhill and took Rock's face with it.

WTF? thought everyone in the theater, including Chris. He quickly looked back up in a state of shock and watched Smith stride back to his seat with a look of smug satisfaction on his face. The crowd was stunned but had no idea if it was real because the whole thing happened too fast for anyone to know. And, let's face it, everything is fake in Hollywood, but especially the people.

"Oh, wow! Wow. Will Smith just smacked the shit out of me," Rock said as the audience laughed nervously.

At this point the "Real-O-Meter" got dialed way up as Smith began shouting from his seat, "Keep my wife's name out your fucking mouth!"

The audience gasped, and Rock responded in disbelief, "Wow, dude!"

Smith shook his head and shot back an angry "*Yes.*"

All the air was sucked out of the room.

This is a thing.

Rock attempted to defuse the situation, downplaying the significance of his comments, telling Smith, "It was a *G.I. Jane* joke."

Having none of it, Will yelled again, but with more feeling because Hollywood, "Keep my wife's name . . . out your fucking *mouth*!"

The room is now aghast, staring in stunned silence.

Rock, to his credit, tried to move on with the show, saying, "I'm going to, okay? Oh, I could, oh, okay. That was a . . . greatest night in the history of television, okay."

The audience responded with a nervous giggle, but the room was quiet enough to hear a pin drop. Thankfully, none of the actresses fell, though.

A few seconds of awkward silence ensued before Rock attempted to settle himself.

"Okay. Okay. So we are here to, uh, give a documentary out. To give an Oscar out for Best Documentary. Because the beauty of documentaries is that they make you feel smart. Like you read a book or something. But all you really did was get high and watch Netflix."

He got a B-plus laugh for this because of the obvious tension in the room and the fact that he was delivering his lines with *a lot* less energy than he was before the attack. Everybody could tell it was impossibly weird for him. This is a guy who murders onstage and he almost got killed.

"So here we go. Here we go. The documentaries. The nominees are . . . Let's just go to the documentaries," he said, shaking his head.

A pre-recorded video came on in which he highlighted the nominees.

When we return to the live feed, Rock opens the envelope, saying, "And the winner is—hooo, I hope this is right—*Summer of Soul (. . . Or, When the Revolution Could Not Be Televised) . . .*"

The crowd cheers as Rock reads off the names of the team who produced it.

"Ahmir 'Questlove' Thompson, Joseph Patel, and four white guys," he jokes as they walk to the stage.

Will Smith can be seen congratulating each winner as they pass his seat, including a big hug for Thompson, who then takes the mic and gives a teary, heartfelt acceptance speech about his late father.

As he speaks, Rock is caught on camera over his shoulder, staring around the room and making a series of bewildered faces as if he's trying to make sense of it all. It's like he just got slapped in front of a few million people or something.

There's plenty of applause to go around during Thompson's speech, but the second he finishes and the orchestra plays the show to commercial, a mad scramble ensues to figure out what the hell happened.

The TV audience still had no idea if it was real, but the incident was exploding on social media. In that first hour alone, footage of the slap became the number one video on YouTube's trending page in over a dozen different countries. The American broadcast had censored out the profanities Smith shouted at Rock, so there was a ton of uncertainty. It wasn't until clips began circulating on Twitter from the uncensored Australian feed that people could see this was visceral anger, and it was absolutely real.

We later came to find out that Kevin Costner, who was waiting offstage to present the next award for Best Director, reportedly told onlookers, "Oh, that was real." Don't take his analysis of Smith and Rock lightly. When you shag as many starlets as Costner has, you become an expert on fake pairs. It's how they came up with the famous line in *Field of Dreams*, "If you build it, he will come."

That may or may not be true, but we do know that, during the commercial break, Smith was comforted by Denzel Washington and Tyler Perry, who'd come over to check on him. According to *Vanity Fair*, all of this went down while Rock was backstage with a visibly red cheek.

Just when you thought the whole thing couldn't get any weirder, out comes the cast of *Pulp Fiction* to present the award for Best Actor. It was one of the most incredible slow-motion train wrecks we will ever witness because this was the category where Will Smith was nominated. As the cast performed their skit, everyone could feel the train chugging toward the broken tracks at the edge of the cliff.

To their credit, Samuel L. Jackson, Uma Thurman, and John Travolta did an excellent job of reenacting some iconic *Pulp Fiction* moments, but the audience was tougher than a three-week-old Royale with Cheese. Sure enough, when they opened the envelope, Will Smith had beaten his fellow actors yet again.

The second his name was called, he popped up faster than a producer on Viagra. He kissed his wife and ran onstage to hug all three presenters as they handed him the trophy. It's hard to tell if the hugs were sincere or if the *Pulp Fiction* cast just wanted to get on his good side, seeing as he was now armed with a weapon.

Zed may be dead, but the rest of them wanted to live.

For what it's worth, the Academy issued a statement the next day claiming it had asked Smith to leave the ceremony after the attack. His camp denied it, but regardless of how it transpired, there he was, accepting the highest individual honor of the night, staring straight into the camera at a time when most people would be getting photographed from the front *and* the side.

Smith wasted no time going after the elephant in the room, seemingly defending his actions by opening with "Oh, man. Richard Williams was a fierce defender of his family."

At which point he began to cry.

Well played.

The guy who saved the world in *Independence Day* was trying to save his ass, and he knew it would take sympathy.

"In this time in my life, in this moment, I am overwhelmed by what God is calling on me to do and be in this world.

"Making this film, I got to protect Aunjanue Ellis, who was one of the most strongest, most delicate people I ever met. I got to protect Saniyya [Sidney] and Demi [Singleton], the two actresses that played Venus and Serena."

As the crowd applauded, you might have wondered how he protected them and from what. After all, they were actors being paid millions of dollars to pretend while surrounded by all kinds of security. Of course, the crowd didn't contemplate any of those things, because there's not a lot of critical thinking in a room full of people who have their words written for them.

The only person in that audience who got a 4.0 in college was Amy Schumer. And that was her blood alcohol content.

Smith continued:

"I'm being called on in my life to love people and to protect people and to be a river to my people.

"Now, I know, to do what we do, you got to be able to take abuse. You got to be able to have people talk crazy about you.

"In this business you got to be able to have people disrespecting you, and you've got to smile and you've got to pretend like that's okay.

"But Richard Williams, and what I loved . . ."

The guy who played the lead in *Concussion* was playing the victim after nearly giving a guy half his size a concussion. There's a shamelessness to it all that's kind of fascinating.

He interrupted himself to respond to words of encouragement from Denzel Washington, which could not be heard by the TV audience.

"Thank you, D," he said, wiping a tear.

"Denzel said to me a few minutes ago, he said, 'At your highest moment, be careful, because that's when the devil comes for you.'"

And the twenty-year-old rappers go for your wife.

He closed by apologizing to the Academy and joking that "love will make you do crazy things."

But apparently love won't make you apologize to Chris Rock for going full Ike Turner on him during your woe-is-me of an acceptance speech.

No matter. The audience gave him a standing ovation as the orchestra played them to commercial, eight bizarre minutes after the speech began.

What's truly amazing—and really does highlight the divide in values between Hollywood and regular people—is that most attendees left that theater thinking the show had hit a high note of redemption.

Maybe it was the starvation in the run-up to the red carpet? Maybe it was the self-preservation instincts in Hollywood that tell you to cozy up to whoever wins the big awards and becomes more powerful in the process? But what the actors framed as a feel-good moment felt like an assault to the rest of the country. Against Chris Rock, no less!

Don't get me wrong: there are plenty of actors Smith could have clobbered that would have gotten him a standing ovation in every living room in America. Talking to you, Mark Ruffalo.

Chris Rock, on the other hand, is beloved, not to mention 130 pounds. So it didn't sit well with the public that the guy who played Muhammad Ali would hit the guy who voiced Marty the Zebra in *Madagascar*. And the fact that he'd receive a standing ovation afterward made less sense to normal people than Hollywood's decision to green-light *The Human Centipede*.

With that said, the Oscars after-parties went on as planned, which was great news for the local drug dealers, male escort services, and morning-after crisis managers. But while Chris Rock was at the Gucci party and Will Smith was at the *Vanity Fair* party, the internet was on fire.

Sensing the PR disaster, the show's producers issued a tweet apologizing for the chaos, saying, *The Academy does not condone violence of any form. Tonight we are delighted to celebrate our 94th Academy Awards winners, who deserve this moment of recognition from their peers and movie lovers around the world.*

Because nothing says *We don't condone violence* like giving a trophy to a guy who just landed a haymaker on national TV.

Millions of memes were making the rounds on social media, and by the time the world woke up Monday morning, the uncensored YouTube video had been seen by over 50 million people.

"The slap heard round the world" was the lead on just about every news show that day. Will Smith once rapped that Parents Just Don't Understand. Well, let the record show that the rest of the country didn't, either. An instant poll by YouGov found that 61 percent of Americans thought it was "totally unacceptable" for him to smack a comedian. Incredibly there were 22 percent who thought the slap was fine. Remind me never to invite those people to a show.

SAG-AFTRA, the labor union representing film and TV actors, issued a statement that morning condemning Smith's behavior, saying:

Violence or physical abuse in the workplace is never appropriate and the union condemns any such conduct. The incident involving Will Smith and Chris Rock at last night's Academy Awards was unacceptable. We have been in contact with the Academy of Motion Picture Arts and Sciences and ABC about this incident and will work to ensure this behavior is appropriately addressed. SAG-AFTRA does not comment on any pending member disciplinary process.

Will Smith can read a script, and he can read a room, so he issued a statement of his own a short while later in which he apologized again to the Academy and also managed to acknowledge Chris Rock this time around:

I would like to publicly apologize to you, Chris. I was out of line and I was wrong. I am embarrassed and my actions were not indicative of the man I want to be. There is no place for violence in a world of love and kindness.

Despite his attempts to put the scandal to bed, new cell phone videos emerged later in the week that kept it wide awake. Some showed the attack from new angles, others showed Rock shaking his head rhythmically after presenting the award for Best Documentary Feature Film. If I didn't know any better, I'd think he was listening to the Weeknd's song "Can't Feel My Face."

On March 30, the Academy announced disciplinary proceedings against Smith for "violations of the Academy's Standards of Conduct, including inappropriate physical contact, abusive or threatening behavior, and compromising the integrity of the Academy."

You know it's bad when the people who covered for Harvey Weinstein are calling you out.

Smith was given fifteen days to issue a written response to the allegations. But rather than doing the homework assignment, he announced on April 1 that he was resigning his membership in the Academy after being informed he would ultimately face a ten-year ban from the Oscars anyway.

For my money, if you really wanna punish the guy, you make him *attend* the ceremony, because going to the Oscars is like doing community service. The only difference is that community service involves picking up trash on the street. At the Oscars, you pick up trash that's seated next to you.

News coverage died down after the ban put a bow on what has to be the most insane thing to ever happen at the Oscars.

Sure, Warren Beatty and Faye Dunaway were given the wrong envelope for the winner of Best Picture at the end of the 2017 ceremony. But when the producers of *La La Land* were told that they had been mistakenly given the award, and that the real winner was *Moonlight*, no crimes were committed in response.

All it amounted to was an awkward acknowledgment of the error, at which point the night ended and the public forgot about it within twenty-four hours.

The slap will be talked about forever.

Jimmy Kimmel mentioned it when he opened the ninety-fifth Oscars the following year, saying, "If anyone in this theater commits an act of violence at any point during the show, you will be awarded the Oscar for best actor and permitted to give a nineteen-minute-long speech."

Funny joke, especially for Kimmel, who is a genuinely capable comic but, like most of Hollywood, has become a little too woke for the world's good.

I say that because there is no doubt the left's propensity for policing speech and treating jokes as genuine attacks played a role in Will Smith storming the stage that night. These are people who take words, and themselves, way too seriously. And although Smith's first instinct was to laugh, the second his wife rolled her eyes as if she'd been victimized, he felt a need to spring into action and avenge her, which makes no sense to normal people.

Dude. You're sitting there being honored, in front of millions of people, with hundreds of millions of dollars in the bank. There's no way you should be that angry about anything, let alone a throwaway joke about your wife.

The crazy part was that if he hadn't attacked Chris Rock, the joke wouldn't have lived beyond the next hour, because nobody would have cared. It was a throwaway line from a routine in which Rock was *crushing* with much bigger subjects.

But living in a world where jokes are treated as violence and swimming in a sea of superegos that treat good-natured kidding as personal attacks, Smith must have felt like his manhood was challenged.

In a normal world, Will would've laughed, and even if Jada hadn't, there would have been no need to announce that she wasn't on board with the joke.

I'll say it again. Comedy is supposed to be treated like a buffet. If you see an item you like, you throw it on your tray. If you don't like the item, you don't have to hold up the whole restaurant by arguing with the staff. Just keep on walking. Everybody gets to throw whatever items they want on their tray.

In Will's case, he climbed over the counter and took a swing at the chef, which is generally frowned upon at most buffets. Even the sketchy ones I was forced to eat at when things went south in my gambling days.

Chris Rock waited a year to speak about the slap in his Netflix special, *Chris Rock: Selective Outrage*. He built toward the moment the entire hour before calling out Smith at the very end for being cheated on and publicly humiliated by his wife. He closed the bit by saying he didn't swing back because he was raised by parents who told him, "Don't fight in front of white people."

It's good advice that nobody ever told the Real Housewives of New Jersey.

All told, the incident was a net-win for Rock, as he sold out every show he did the following year and raised his ticket prices in the process, due to overwhelming interest in the slap.

Will Smith, on the other hand, is still on the outs with polite society, but he'll be fine in the long run. If Chris Brown can come back and win a Grammy after assaulting a woman, there's no question Will Smith can rebound from clocking a comedian.

But don't cry for Will, because the dude made a gazillion bucks and he'll get by without you starting a GoFundMe account.

And I'm pretty sure most people are going to take his advice and "keep his wife's name out of their fucking mouths." Although, if history is any indicator, I'm not sure they'll keep the rest of his wife's body out of their mouths.

Just a joke, folks. Please stay seated and keep your hands to yourself.

Tim Allen and Tiger Woods

Tim Allen and Tiger Woods don't have a heck of a whole lot in common. Allen is famous for his voice-over work in *Toy Story*. Tiger was not in *Toy Story*, although he did get in trouble for having a buzz and a woody.

Heyyyo! There it is! Pow!

Despite their vastly different backgrounds, the two did manage to briefly become neighbors in Cancel Town, U.S.A. Although their offenses were completely different, which I just want to point out in case Tim Allen's wife is reading this. Let's just say that if Tiger Woods was in a Pixar film, it would be called *Grinding Nemo*.

Tim Allen, on the other hand, is a man who rose to fame in Hollywood despite the fact that he once got busted at a Michigan airport with a pound and a half of cocaine. But when he tried to portray a likable conservative on TV, Hollywood decided he had crossed the line. Although, in his case, I guess that was better than what he used to do with the line.

This one begins in May 2017. Allen, who became a household name in the '90s for playing with tools on *Home Improvement*, was enjoying a second act in the sitcom world on a well-rated show called *Last Man Standing*. The Friday-night show was in its sixth season, averaging a solid 8.3 million viewers in its time slot, and had just won the previous week's ratings battle when ABC sent America's favorite tool guy to that big Home Depot in the sky.

This was a weird one out of the gate. Sure, TV shows get canceled all the time, and if you don't believe me, ask Don Lemon. What made this one different than, say, Lemon's is that people watched it. A hit show getting canceled is like Joe Biden completing a sentence. It happens, but it's rare.

I'm telling cheap jokes about liberals because the fact that Tim Allen wasn't one of them seems to be the only reason ABC let him go.

He summed up the cancellation on a podcast hosted by the late great Norm Macdonald, saying it wasn't just the character he played on-screen but the character he was off-screen:

"Archie Bunker pushed boundaries, but Carroll O'Connor [the man who played him] was not that guy at all. I *am* a version of that guy. But there is nothing more dangerous, especially in this climate, than a funny, likable conservative character."

The climate he was referring to was the very beginning of the Trump administration, when the media pretended Trump was a Russian agent and Hollywood actors pretended to be political experts, bashing Trump in every speech, tweet, and Instagram video they could.

I know we discussed it earlier in the book, but there is no understating just how hysterical Hollywood got after Trump's inauguration. If actors were cats, Trump was fifty laser pointers. Whenever he opened his mouth, he sent them scrambling frantically in every direction. I'm pretty sure they even coughed up a few fur balls, although it could've been the eating disorders.

For a time, it seemed like anyone who accepted an award was contractually obligated to call Trump a racist for wanting a wall at the southern border, which of course resulted in huge applause from entire theaters full of people who had walls around their mansions. It looked damn silly to outsiders, but it was dead serious in Hollywood, which had to influence ABC's decision to cut the only openly conservative actor in town.

The network denied reports that politics played a role, but that day's write-up on the cancellation in *Variety*, aka the Hollywood Bible, seemed to tell a different story.

Speaking to the ratings for *Last Man Standing*, *Variety* stated:

The domestic comedy produced by 20th Century Fox TV was a durable player for the network in the Friday 8 p.m. berth, and it has been a solid performer for 20th TV in syndication.

So we weren't exactly dealing with a flop so much as a political outlier that nobody in Hollywood wanted to own in that political climate.

Here's the portion of *Variety*'s article that tells you everything you need to know:

"Last Man Standing" was ahead of the curve in the cultural sense as Allen played a conservative-minded patriarch who runs a sporting goods store and opines about the modern world, including political topics such as Obamacare and environmental policy.

Translation: This show portrays a conservative as likable and non-threatening. Any Hollywood executive who continues to support it could lose everything in this town. That would be a disaster not only for the executive and his family but also for the second family in the valley that his first family doesn't know about.

I'm not a Hollywood producer, but as a former cabdriver, I sometimes feel like one, given the amount of time I spent around drugs and prostitutes on a daily basis.

But for my money I could never understand why anyone would avoid programming that appeals to 50 percent of potential TV viewers. It seems like you're shooting yourself in the foot, and, let's face it, nobody wants to get shot *anywhere*, which is why they avoid working on Alec Baldwin films.

Looking back at the cancellation of *Last Man Standing*, it seems like studios might have been working a long con in that they needed the anti-Trump fury to die down before they went back to acknowledging that not all conservatives carpool to work with Satan.

I say that because *Yellowstone* is as big as anything that's hit a TV screen in the past decade, and Kevin Costner's character, John Dutton, wasn't exactly going out of his way to use the preferred pronouns of the tribal leaders he battled. Nor was Cole Hauser's character, Rip, driving an eco-friendly car when he "took people to the train station" to kill them.

Even so, the show's executive producer, Taylor Sheridan, said he couldn't get *Yellowstone* made when HBO held the rights during the Trump years. A top executive at the network reportedly told him the show was "too middle America."

That's code for blue-collar people who don't force a social engineering agenda on every establishment they frequent, which is a big no-no in the virtue-signaling hamster wheel of Hollywood. Sheridan recounted the struggle to get the show made during an interview with the *Hollywood Reporter* in June 2023, saying:

"We go to lunch in some snazzy place in West L.A. And John Linson [*Yellowstone* co-creator] finally asks: 'Why don't you want to make it?'

"And the HBO VP goes: 'Look, it just feels so Middle America. We're HBO, we're avant-garde, we're trendsetters. This feels like a step backwards. And frankly, I've got to be honest with you, I don't think anyone should be living out there [in rural Montana]. It should be a park or something.'"

Now, granted, there are definitely two different lifestyles in Montana and LA. One is filled with wildlife that's hunting for food all day and killing each other at night. And the other is Montana.

See what I did there?

These days the executives at HBO who passed on the show want to kill themselves. *Yellowstone* has been a monster success, spawning multiple prequels and now a spin-off coming with Matthew McConaughey. I believe that one's called *Yellowstoned*.

As for Tim Allen, he seems to be back in Hollywood's good graces as he's set to reprise his role as Buzz Lightyear in the upcoming *Toy Story* film. But let the record show that Hollywood once told a man who played a talking toy and starred in *The Santa Clause* that having a likable conservative was too big of a fantasy.

Tiger Woods had some fantasies of his own, and reportedly acted a few of them out with a waitress from a Perkins Restaurant. This was just one of over a dozen affairs that surfaced after Woods's then wife, Elin Nordegren, quite literally teed off on his Cadillac Escalade when she found out the world's top golfer had been playing a few extra holes.

Ahem.

In November 2009, with Woods on top of the golf world and raking in over $40 million a year in endorsements, anything this guy did was a big deal. So when a photo surfaced on TMZ showing Woods with a scratched face, the story quickly blew up everywhere else on the internet. Woods's camp claimed he sustained the lacerations after he drove his Cadillac Escalade into a fire hydrant in a distracted driving accident that was caused by several pain medications he was taking. Seeing as we had no history of Tiger being untruthful, let alone undressed, the public seemed to take him at his word—at least for a few hours, anyway.

The original TMZ report included photos of the vehicle. One of the captions was:

"Remnants of debris can be seen scattered across the driveway—possibly from when Tiger's wife smashed out the back window to help him."

TMZ was accurate in saying his wife smashed out the back window, but this was not the work of a Good Samaritan trying to free a guy from a car wreck. No, according to TMZ's follow-up report, it turns out Woods's wife had confronted him in the driveway of their home about his side chicks, an argument ensued, and the man who became a "scratch golfer" at the age of thirteen became a very scratched golfer.

Woods attempted to flee the scene in the Escalade, at which point she grabbed one of his golf clubs and bashed the windows as he drove away.

It was then that Woods got distracted and hit the fire hydrant, causing a small portion of the damage we'd later see in the TMZ photos. The rest of the destruction was caused by his wife, who apparently did not consider their marriage to be the U.S. Open.

Tiger was easily the most famous athlete in the world at the time, so the media circus that ensued quickly became the greatest show on earth.

Dozens of women came forward after news broke of Woods's extramarital action, including the aforementioned Perkins waitress, Mindy Lawton, who said she and Woods regularly saw each other for sex in his car, which was parked in a church parking lot.

Praise the Lord (and pass the lube)!

Then came word that one of Woods's back seat bogies was caught on film by photographers working for the *National Enquirer*. The UK's *Daily Mirror* tabloid reported that the *Enquirer* story was buried after Woods agreed to appear on the cover of *Men's Fitness*, which was owned by the *Enquirer*'s parent company, American Media. It was a quid pro quo, but Tiger was in bigger trouble for the quid pro ho, if you will.

There were so many women coming forward in those first few days that the question quickly went from "How many more?" to "How did he ever keep this quiet?"

One way was to have women sign nondisclosure agreements like the one Woods reportedly reached with Las Vegas event promoter Rachel Uchitel, whose alleged relationship with Woods was famously outed by the media in 2009. The women who didn't have NDAs did have plenty of text messages and even a few voicemails.

A Vegas cocktail waitress named Jaimee Grubbs shared a message Woods purportedly left in which he asked her to quickly take her name off her own voicemail greeting for fear that his wife might call:

> *Hey, it's Tiger. I need you to do me a huge favor. Can you please, uh, take your name off your phone? My wife went through my phone and may be calling you. If you can, please take your name off that and, um, what do you call it, just have it as a number on the voicemail. Just have it as your telephone number. You have to do this for me. Huge. Quickly. Bye.*

Grubbs also shared over three hundred text messages, which inspired the Woods camp to release a vague statement owning his behavior in an attempt to stop the public relations nightmare that was unfolding for Tiger and his sponsors.

> *I have let my family down and I regret those transgressions with all of my heart. I have not been true to my values and the behavior my fam-*

ily deserves. I am not without faults and I am far short of perfect. I am dealing with my behavior and personal failings behind closed doors with my family. Those feelings should be shared by us alone.

Unfortunately for Tiger, that was not the end of the side-chick stampede as he continued to be linked to even more women, including an adult film actress named Holly Sampson, who starred in a porno called *Flying Solo 2*.

It's worth noting that, as movies go, *Flying Solo 2* is one of the rare sequels that's better than the original. Don't get me wrong, it's no *Horny Housewives 3* or *Nympho Nurses 6*, but it's still a damn good film. If you're wondering these films are no longer available for sale. But you can probably get the X-rated book if you have a kindergartner in a liberal school district.

But back to Tiger, who seemed to be playing a game called Duck, Duck, Grey Goose as he partied his way through America's nightclubs. There were so many women coming forward, it was impossible to know what was real and what was tabloid sensationalism. But one thing was clear: Woods's reputation as a clean-cut family man was completely destroyed, and his sponsors seemed to notice.

Gatorade was one of the first brands to drop him, and then AT&T and Accenture quickly followed suit. Gillette also decided to shave down their payroll, as did luxury watchmaker TAG Heuer. The endorsement cancellations were said to cost Woods $34 million. But it's hard to count because he got paid in singles.

What we do know for sure is that by the end of 2010 his only remaining sponsors were Nike and EA Sports video games. His wife was also long gone, filing for divorce in August of that year and receiving over $100 million in a settlement. There were reports that the number reached as high as $750 million, but we'll never know for sure because, like many of her husband's mistresses, Elin Nordegren also signed a nondisclosure as part of the divorce settlement.

It was an absolutely stunning fall for a man who was by far the biggest athlete in the world, but it was hardly the end of Tiger. Yes, his family-friendly reputation was ruined and his career was derailed by injuries for half a decade. There was also a 2017 DUI arrest in which he allegedly had five different drugs in his system.

But he did eventually come roaring back to win the Masters again in 2019. It was his fifth Masters Tournament win and his first since the divorce sent his reputation into a sand trap back in 2010. In the years since the Masters win, the advertisers have come back, too, with Woods pulling in an estimated $68 million in 2022 from companies like Nike, Bridgestone, Monster Energy, and Rolex. And he also got to play golf against the greatest golfer in history, if you believe what Donald Trump says about himself.

The good news for Tiger is the money is rolling in again. The bad news is he'll need the cash because a new legal battle broke out in May 2023 with his latest ex, Erica Herman. She sued to get out of yet another NDA from Tiger, who apparently likes using his lawyers just as much as his ladies. Seriously, for all the companies who chose him as a spokesperson, I feel like there was a major missed opportunity with LegalZoom. Who knows, maybe they'll pick him up in the coming years, as Tiger will likely have even more lovers' quarrels in the court system. But don't be surprised if it all works out in his favor. After all, if we've learned anything in this chapter, it's that every Tiger Woods story has a happy ending.

U

Universities

In November 2019, a group of climate protesters stormed onto the football field during "the Game" between Harvard and Yale. Police let them run all the way to the end zone, presumably because this was the only time any of them was ever going to score.

It's unclear why the climate crowd did it. These were two of the most liberal schools in the world, meaning pretty much everyone in the bleachers agreed with their position on the climate but disagreed with their position on the field. Regardless, the protest lasted forty minutes before the players from Harvard and Yale could get back to doing what they do best, which is selling term papers to the players at good football schools.

Universities have always been a bug light for peculiar protests. Students at Cornell University once held a "cry-in" to deal with the election of Donald Trump. It went nowhere because, let's face it, if America wanted to watch people cry over Donald Trump, CNN would have much higher ratings.

The University of Texas at Austin once staged a "Cocks Not Glocks" protest in which students strapped dildos to their backpacks to protest the state's open-carry law. The bad news is hundreds of students ended up in handcuffs afterward. The good news is there was fur on them.

I think my favorite protest of all time, for all the wrong reasons, was when students at the University of Amherst in Massachusetts organized something called a "shit-in." The invite urged participants to sit on campus toilets for a week to protest the lack of gender-neutral bathrooms.

I don't even know what to say to the shit-in crowd because stuff like this didn't happen at the community college I attended.

Nope.

The only time our students protested was when the bar ran out of beer on Nickel Beer Night. And the only time we'd sit for a week on the toilet was after drinking the sludge they served at Nickel Beer Night.

I'm telling you because I care, folks. There are certain things in life you don't want to buy if they're too cheap. Everybody thinks those ads for $50 laser eye surgery seem like a really good deal until the cross-eyed doctor walks in to operate on you. Let's just say that Nickel Beer Night is the $50 laser eye surgery of drinking. Although you'll wish you were blind when you see who you wake up in bed with the next morning.

As a comedian who tours the country and sells a lot more tickets than a man of my talents should—*thank you, Fox News*—I've watched up close as colleges transformed from free-thought factories teaching students *how* to think into conformity cops that teach students *what* to think. And it's changed the vibe at stand-up shows big-time.

When I was about to go onstage at a student center in say, 2005, the campus activities committee would urge you to plug the movie or whatever group event that was taking place in the lion's den after your set. Fast-forward ten years, and the list of things they wanted you to say was one-tenth as long as the list of things they *didn't* want you to say for fear of upsetting someone and getting us all fed to the lions. Everything is off-limits. Politics, race, religion, gender, sexual orientation, cats, dogs, even cats who identify as dogs. At this point you're better off telling the school that your jokes identify as "inoffensive" and backing them into a corner. Let's face it, none of these wokesters wanna look like bigots for banning someone who's transfensive.

Frankly, watching them put all of this emotional bubble wrap around college kids is a sad thing to see.

I also find it sad that I said the word "frankly," but in my defense it's one of the few terms I can still use at a college without getting in trouble. (Assuming there isn't a guy named Frank in the news today for doing something bad, in which case I apologize for the hurt I caused and promise to educate myself and do better.)

We're living in the dumbest time ever, and the deterioration of free thought on college campuses has led the way in getting us there.

What's crazy is that it wasn't always this way. Like, not even close!

Colleges used to be these cool countercultural bastions of sex, drugs, and rock and roll. A home for the rugged individualism of people striving to stand out. As opposed to today's tribal, woke day cares where students just fight to *fit in*.

I can't even begin to tell you how foreign this is to me, because when I was a kid, the most iconic stand-up comedy special on HBO was a 1984 classic called *George Carlin: Carlin on Campus*. The premise of the special was that George Carlin's act was so thought-provoking that he *had to* shoot it at UCLA because college kids were the only people who could have their beliefs challenged without freaking out. Meaning they were the toughest crowds to offend.

I know, this is harder to imagine than Casey Anthony landing a job at a day care, but college crowds used to be the absolute best. No joke went too far, and the only time you heard the words "Too soon" was when you finished in some girl's dorm. They weren't bringing in puppies to help kids cope with stress the way they do today. Don't get me wrong: kids did get super stressed in the '80s and '90s. The difference is our relief outlets were smoked from a bong or drunk from one of the twenty-four cans of liquid that came in a cardboard case. No, I'm not talking about *Coke*; I'm talking about the *beer* that was in every fridge. The coke was on the coffee table, if you're picking up what I'm putting down in the Ziploc bag they just found in the White House.

Sure, there's plenty of college kids partying today, but for every dude doing a keg stand, there are ten dorks using the stress relief coloring books that many schools now hand out for traumatized students. Yes, that's a thing.

To which I say, Dude. *You're in* college. *The only time you should be using a Magic Marker is when your buddy passes out drunk. I'm telling you because I care.* The era of incentivized grievance has wound these kids way too tight.

Consider this:

George Carlin: Carlin on Campus began with a video sketch in which the comedian played both a nun and a male student who gets kicked out of class for being disruptive. As he enters the hallway, the student looks into the camera and tells viewers that he's glad he got ejected because he's now free to go where he's always wanted to go. He's then shown entering the girls' bathroom.

It got a huge laugh because, in 1984, the idea of a biological man entering a women's bathroom was considered ridiculous for a whole variety of reasons. As it was ten years later in 1994, and again in 2004 and 2014. But hold it right there, because if Carlin pulled this stunt in 2024, the blowback would make the atomic bomb look like a sparkler.

My word! Making fun of a man using the women's room?

There'd be *at least* a good month's worth of *shit-ins*.

The student audience raucously applauded his guy-in-the-girls'-room sketch as Carlin walked onto the stage and launched right into several jokes about the AIDS epidemic. Those bits crushed, too, because back then students knew the difference between a joke and a genocide. And it was cooler to laugh at life's adversities than it was to fold your arms and frown, thinking of all the people that you could get offended on behalf of.

You see, colleges used to teach kids that their right to free expression entitled them to laugh at everything they found funny and question anything they didn't agree with. Nowadays the only question schools want you to ask is: What's the best way to ruin anyone who disagrees with our thesis that America is a racist, sexist, oppressive hellhole?

Woke colleges no longer support Martin Luther King Jr.'s dream of his children living in "a nation where they will not be judged by the color of their skin but by the content of their character." No, the modern student activist wants segregated graduation ceremonies, which is exactly what happened on seventy-five campuses in 2019, including those of Harvard, UC San Diego, UC Irvine, Arizona State University, Stanford, UC Berkeley, UCLA, and Yale.

That number has only grown in the aftermath of the Black Lives Matter protests and, incredibly, all this neo-segregation is being pushed by people who call themselves "progressives."

I'm *telling you*, this is the dumbest time there has ever been to be alive.

Student activism got its legs in the '60s and '70s on campuses that protested our military involvement in Vietnam. Yet somehow the generation who started the "Make Love, Not War" movement has been succeeded by kids who won't make love unless you support the war in Ukraine.

I can't imagine how insane it must be to the people who gathered on the campus quad to scream at the government to watch their descendants go all in on crushing anyone who questions the government's agenda. But that's exactly where we are on wars, vaccines, and climate change—and heaven forbid someone takes a stance against Big Pronoun, whose advocates literally fight for tolerance by assaulting people who disagree with it.

Nobody knows this better than Riley Gaines, a star female swimmer at the University of Pennsylvania who began speaking out against the unfair practice of biological men competing in women's sports.

She'd seen the injustice firsthand after Will Thomas, a male swimmer who was ranked 462nd in the country, announced that he was now a female named Lia Thomas and quickly shot all the way up to number one in the women's rankings. Not only was Lia Thomas the first swimmer in history to make such a meteoric rise, she was the first woman to battle her opponents while also battling shrinkage.

Gaines would later tell Congress that members of the women's swimming team were under immense social pressure to go along with Thomas's addition because anyone who expressed contrarian views was immediately labeled a hateful bigot and a transphobe.

So her teammates spent the season changing in the same locker room as a biological man who frequently exposed his genitalia despite the fact that the university never asked for their consent. Not wanting to look intolerant, Gaines and the girls played ball until they realized the only views not being tolerated were their own.

Riley quickly went viral after she began to speak out, likely because polls say most of society agrees with her position that biological men have too big an advantage against biological women.

The winner of the New York City men's marathon is *fifteen minutes faster* than the winner of the women's marathon. And again, that's in *New York*, where every woman runs extra fast because they're usually being chased.

There was a time when this sort of thing was okay to acknowledge, as Serena Williams once did on *Late Night with David Letterman*. During a 2013 interview about the state of tennis, Dave asked Serena, the most dominant women's tennis player of all time, if she'd accept an invitation to play against her good friend Andy Murray.

Her response:

"If I were to play Andy Murray, I would lose 6–0, 6–0 in five to six minutes, maybe ten minutes. No, it's true. It's a completely different sport. The men are a lot faster, and they serve harder, they hit harder. It's just a different game. I love to play women's tennis. I only want to play girls, because I don't want to be embarrassed."

The crowd laughed and applauded the candor she showed in acknowledging such an obvious truth. If Williams said this today, she'd be called a transphobic bigot, and Nike would be under pressure to sever any and all ties with her family.

Why is this happening, Jimbo?

(For some reason, I picture you as the type of person who'd call me Jimbo.)

The modern student activists and their friends in the outrage mob have created a massive divide between what people believe to be true and what they're willing to say in public. And faced with the irrational level of blowback that comes from disagreeing, most people and companies play along to avoid a stampede of self-righteousness that could kill their careers or their company. For that reason, it's highly doubtful Serena would admit any of the things she said on *Letterman* today, not because they aren't true but because they aren't safe. But, folks, if the truth ain't safe, then neither are we.

Which is why you have to applaud a female athlete like Riley Gaines. Thankfully, many people did. And as she continued to speak out, she exploded in popularity. So much so that she began appearing regularly on prime-time cable news shows, where she even got to hobnob with *major* media figures like myself.

You laugh, but I am technically the 347th most powerful person at

Fox News. Whoops! As I was writing this, I just read a headline that Geraldo left the network. Mark me down as the 346th most powerful person here, and wish Geraldo luck wherever he goes next.

Fine. You don't have to. But I still will.

In April 2023, Riley Gaines traveled to San Francisco State University to speak with a campus group about the right for biological women to compete on a level playing field. It's worth noting that this is exactly what student activists fought for in passing Title IX exactly fifty years ago, but now they're all the way against it.

Gaines would later testify to Congress about the day's speech, saying the school had told her they'd send over campus police to brief her on a security plan before the event started. Unfortunately, the cops didn't show up, but the protesters turned out in full force, which doesn't surprise me because there's not much to do in San Francisco these days besides marveling at the empty storefronts downtown, stepping on a syringe in Union Square, and getting chased by a hobbit in the Tenderloin. Don't get me wrong, all these activities are fabulous fun for the whole family, but they do get old after a while.

Gaines made it onstage without incident, only to have a mob storm in during her speech, flicker the lights, and shout her down.

As the room filled with anarchy, she looked for a path out, at which point a biological male introduced himself as a security guard and urged her to follow him. She did, only to have him hit her and try to drag her further into the crowd. She ran out of the class and was chased down a hallway before she retreated to a different classroom, barricaded herself inside, and called for help.

Thankfully, the San Francisco Police Department eventually arrived and was able to get her out but not before she was cursed at, spit on, and hit by the people who claim to stand for tolerance.

As you'd imagine, this incident was abhorrent enough for the university to issue an apology. But in the ultimate WTF moment, the school apologized to the attackers and not their victim!

True story. Four days after video of the incident went viral, San Francisco State University president Lynn Mahoney issued a statement that said,

> *Last Thursday, Turning Point USA hosted an event on campus that advocated for the exclusion of trans people in athletics. The event was deeply traumatic for many in our trans and LGBTQ+ communities, and the speaker's message outraged many members of the SF State community. To our trans community, please know how welcome you are. We will turn this moment into an opportunity to listen and learn about how we can better support you.*

Forget the girl who was shouted down, beaten up, and held for ransom. We need to give the people who did it more support! I'm assuming the school means brass knuckles or nunchucks to make the next attack easier?

The truth is if you really wanted to help college kids, and the country as a whole, we'd bring back the ability to have substantive conversations without labeling any form of disagreement a "hateful call to violence." But that's exactly what's happening at universities all across the country.

What were once proud bastions of free expression are now governed by hive-minded social justice crusaders who frame dissenting views as violence, which in their mind, justifies a proportional response. The way they see it, conservatives like Riley Gaines are hateful bigots trying to harm trans athletes, so why not literally beat them to the punch?

Meanwhile, back here in reality, *nobody*, literally not a single person anywhere, is saying trans people shouldn't have access to athletics. We're saying all athletes should compete against people of the same biological gender because we have overwhelming proof that men have advantages over women. It doesn't mean we hate trans people or want someone to attack them. And it doesn't mean we're against inclusion.

The whole point of America is to *do you*.

Freedom.

This country was founded under the principle of *e pluribus unum*, which means "out of many, we are one."

But if we're going to live up to our doctrine of fairness for all, then we have to protect biological women, because throwing them in the ring against biological men isn't fair. That position is not anti-trans; it's simply pro-women. Yet Riley Gaines and hundreds of other conservative speakers continue to be met with protests and actual violence for disagreeing with Team Tolerance.

They talk about tolerance like it requires you to silence people you don't agree with. But to quote the great swordsman Inigo Montoya in *The Princess Bride*, "You keep using that word, I do not think it means what you think it means."

Apparently nobody corrected the nine people arrested at Berkeley College after they attempted to shut down a Ben Shapiro speech in 2017. Although to their credit, this was better than the previous year's Berkeley Bunch, who set the campus on fire to protest the arrival of right-wing speaker Milo Yiannopoulos. I mean, who needs free speech when you've got a free book of matches?

Two of my conservative colleagues and frequent radio guests have also been met with major protests in recent years.

Katie Pavlich, who's one of the best all-around humans you could ever hope to come across, is a big advocate of Second Amendment rights for women. She's also way into fashion and has the top boot collections in television. On the radio we refer to her as a General in the Failla Fashion Army, but her true superpower is that she's crazy funny and supersmart. When you see her on Fox News, you'll also notice she has a better grasp on the gun issue than anybody who's ever strapped a dildo to their backpacks to protest the Second Amendment.

In October 2017, Katie was booked at the University of Wisconsin–Madison to speak on behalf of a woman's right to self-defense. When news reached the local "Cocks Not Glocks" group, they organized something called a "Bonerfide Penis Arts Fest." It encouraged signs of "dick art that has ZERO literary, artistic, political, educational, or scientific value." You know, as opposed to all the "dick art" that does have literary, artistic, political, educational, and scientific value? I mean, everybody remembers where they were the first time they saw a painting by Pablo Pi*cock*so.

But just when you thought it couldn't get any more ridiculous, emphasis on *dic*, the organizers followed in the footsteps of previous "Cocks Not Glocks" movements and encouraged attendees to tie dildos to their backpacks. Seriously, what's with all the dildo protests in the anti-gun crowd? Like, I get that you don't support our Second Amendment right to "a well regulated Militia." But it doesn't mean we should replace them with a well-penetrated one.

Thankfully Katie's speech went off without any violence, although many people who watched the protests undoubtedly wanted to harm themselves.

Seriously, what do you chant when you're marching around campus with a dildo in your hand?

"What do we want? Lube! When do we want it? Now!"

I can't with these people.

Tomi Lahren is another badass buddy of mine whom liberals hate for her outspokenness. That being said, if you met her, you'd love her. She's got a great sense of humor and loves to mock all the performative stupidity in the world because deep down we all do. On a side note, she's talked to me about Bravo shows so much that I sometimes feel like a straight Andy Cohen. If you're wondering why I say "sometimes," you've never seen my wardrobe.

Tomi was supposed to speak at the University of New Mexico in September 2022, but when she showed up the student protesters went all "Real Housewife" on her and began cursing and throwing stuff. She was ultimately forced to evacuate after the state police decided to shut down her speech for safety purposes, meaning they were protecting her from the "tolerant" crowd.

Hundreds of conservatives have been greeted on campus by Antifa groups who claim to be fighting fascism by stifling the speech rights of people they don't agree with. Because nothing says you're against dictatorships like silencing your opponents with violence. It's like saying you're against gambling and you hold a poker tournament to raise money for the cause.

That's the saddest thing about today's campus culture warriors: they possess such a stunning lack of self-awareness. Whereas yesterday's students were opposing wars and taking rebellious stances in classic stick-it-to-the-Man fashion, everything today's kids are fighting for is already supported by the Man.

You're not a rebel if you're standing up for the same agenda as the HR office, your professors, the army brass, or the editorial page of the *New York Times*. And you're not oppressed if you can banish any speaker who's not with you in the battle against pretend oppression.

Yeah, student activism is bigger than ever on our nation's college campuses. But what started as a fight for free speech in the '60s has morphed into a censorship crusade that aspiring dictators will study to hone their craft. The good news for the woke mafia is that all these *shit-ins* and *dildo parades* have gotten them the power to ban anyone who tells an off-color joke.

The bad news is they've become one.

Victoria's Secret

When Victoria's Secret canceled its catalog in May 2016, it didn't make big headlines because by then most women were shopping for clothes online. That being said, it was still surprising to see it go, because the male readers had a lot of pull.

Don't you dare judge that joke: we had to make one somewhere.

If anything, I tried to wrap things up quickly like all the guys who snuck these catalogs into the bathroom over the years.

As tough as this might be for anyone under the age of forty to imagine, there was a time when human beings did not have twenty-four-hour access to every type of pornography you could dream of—not to mention a lot of types that you couldn't and even shouldn't dream of. But I'm not here to shame your tastes or the jobs you may have taken over the years to get by. After all, the rent don't pay itself.

All I'm saying is, for an older generation of men, finding this collection of scantily clad women in the mailbox meant they were *definitely* getting some that night, even if they were doing it alone.

Unfortunately for all these handsy hombres, the parent company of Victoria's Secret, L Brands, was trying to take care of business in a different way. They held the annual smut shipment to the time-honored financial standard of *If it don't make dollars, it don't make sense*. And the catalog did not make them a single dollar in profit, although it would have made them billions of them if they got a kickback from the hand cream companies.

Unlike some of the other products that got whacked in this book, the catalog didn't meet its maker as a direct response to the outrage mob. But if you look a little closer, you'll see that while the social pressure squad didn't outright kill the catalog, they undoubtedly hastened its demise and nuked the company's world-famous runway show along the way.

This one began in 2013, when Victoria's Secret unveiled a new marketing slogan called "I Love My Body" that claimed to be pushing the need for self-acceptance. A fine message, to be sure, because the truth is we should all learn to love our bodies. And I say this as a dude who's not exactly a model for Banana Republic. If anything, I'm more Banana Split.

The internet agreed with the slogan but was absolutely not okay with the fact that the campaign only featured women that looked perfect by society's standards as it would seem impossible for them *not* to love their bodies. Now, it goes without saying that, sadly, women of all shapes and sizes have issues with their bodies and develop eating disorders. Still, the cancel crowd interacts with nuanced issues as well as a bathtub interacts with a toaster.

In the eyes of the mob, Victoria's Secret was guilty of shaping a national mindset that only skinny women can be considered "Runway-Worthy." And they were accused of giving women an even bigger complex by airbrushing the photos in their ads to make the women appear even sexier than they were in real life.

This is a heavy subject, in more ways than one, but I have to say that I always find it funny when people attack a company for photoshopping images to make them more attractive. Especially when you consider that every single picture people post on social media is edited within an inch of its life to make them look as good as humanly possible.

Seriously, when you think about just how much filtering and photoshopping goes into an Instagram post, the app should have the tagline "This Is What I'd Look Like if I Was WAY Hotter."

We're all guilty of false advertising in pictures, but the argument against Victoria's Secret enhancing women's appearances is that they're always doing it as a means of making women look a certain way, i.e., thinner and curvier. I do understand where some women are coming from on this one. As a chubby dude, I never see a men's clothing model who looks like he gets paid in bourbon and buffalo wings. These days, the only way for me to see an overweight biological white guy in a commercial is if he's modeling female clothes.

I've never felt the need to bash advertisers who didn't show my type because I never got my self-worth from commercials, and neither did anyone else until social media made it trendy to look at ourselves as victims and blame society for all of our shortcomings.

Which is why I don't buy into the notion that Victoria's Secret or, say, the *Sports Illustrated* swimsuit issue truly does shape our preferences when it comes to how women look.

Tens of millions of men and women are looking for "dad bods" and "thick girls." The gals who fall into this category get hit on *all the time*. And if you don't think so, you never hung out with me in college.

And if the internet has taught us anything, it's that no matter what you look like, there is someone who looks exactly like you selling naked pictures of themselves, and it's working.

I didn't need a lingerie catalog to tell me "plus-sized women" were fantastic, and neither did any of the chubby-chasers who hit on me. Same goes for the people buying the naked pictures online. Half of these weirdos couldn't even get a catalog in the mail because they live in their cars. For that reason, I have a hard time believing that, by including only skinny chicks in their fashion shows, Victoria's Secret was somehow costing "plus-sized women" any desirability points whatsoever. The existence of Chris Hemsworth didn't keep the woman of my dreams from marrying me. Although it does explain why she always wants me to use an Australian accent in the sack.

Of course, the internet didn't quite agree with my sentiments, and Victoria's Secret caught holy hell for the lack of inclusion in its "I Love My Body" ads.

The blowback wasn't big enough to cancel the 2013 campaign, but it definitely stigmatized the mail-order catalog enough that by 2016 those models were walking the plank instead of the runway. The last thing a company needs is to spend $150 million for the privilege of being called a bunch of body shamers. Take it from a guy who's spent a little time on Craigslist: you can get somebody to demean you for *much* cheaper than that.

After decades of featuring only traditional models like Heidi Klum, Gisele Bündchen, and Stephanie Seymour, the angels spread their wings in 2019 by hiring their first plus-sized model and their first transgender model.

Of course, there were still some cries that the models weren't "plus-sized enough." Which begs the question: Did they want the gal in the French maid outfit to put down the feather duster and pick up a turkey leg? No matter. The good news for the company was that they looked a lot more inclusive to *most* of their critics. The bad news was at the cash register.

After revising its lineup, the brand posted a net loss of $72 million in 2020. Some of that was undoubtedly attributable to the pandemic closing stores, but even after malls fully reopened, their overall sales were still down 6.4 percent in 2022.

It would be wrong to blame their decline on the new additions to their lineup, because in fairness the lingerie market has become way more competitive since Victoria's Secret launched in 1977. The advent of the internet has fueled the rise of lingerie giants at Amazon, Savage X Fenty, and even Kim Kardashian's new line, Skims, which has allowed us to see Kim as we've never seen her before: with clothes on.

But there's no way to claim that making the models more relatable has boosted business for Victoria's Secret. Sales remain down, and it can't help that a brand that became famous for standing out is now doing everything it can to fit in.

This is my biggest problem with the woke marketing executives who try to placate every backlash from the grievance gang. Often, doing so requires them to distance their brands from what always worked in the first place.

Think back to Bud Light for a minute. They sold a gajillion dollars' worth of beer—were literally the number one brand in the world—while pumping their commercials full of bros being bros. Walking away from that focus for a single Dylan Mulvaney can—an influencer who would freely admit to being the least bro-iest person on earth—destroyed the most iconic beer brand in the world.

Over $20 billion worth of financial carnage—totally avoidable if the company just stuck to what made them successful. Unfortunately for them, a social justice crusader bamboozled the boardroom with a bunch of buzzwords and got them to "freshen up the brand," which is code for "alienate anyone who likes it."

I'm not saying Victoria's Secret went the Bud Light route, but there is no question they've gotten away from what made them huge, all to be accepted by the people who yell the loudest.

And again, I get that other types of women want to be included and

I am your biggest cheerleader. If you don't believe me, check my search history. It may or may not include the phrase "biggest cheerleader."

My point is Victoria's Secret became the biggest lingerie retailer in the world not by catering to inclusion but by doing something so exclusive that it legitimately broke the internet the first time they streamed their annual fashion show online.

True story. So many people tried logging in during the opening minute of the 1999 show that it crashed the servers completely. Fortunately for the company, they were eventually able to get the traffic under control, mainly because most of the male viewers only needed to watch for a few minutes.

That being said, the crash only heightened the brand's rock star street cred, and the company leaned all the way into its status as the Mount Olympus of mammaries.

The 2000 show kicked off with Gisele Bündchen walking the runway in what was then the most expensive piece of lingerie ever created, a $15 million diamond-and-ruby-encrusted "Fantasy Bra." There were rhinestone thongs and golden teddies, and as the show got gaudier over the years, so did the money, with profits soaring by 70 percent between 2006 and 2015.

The company continued to catch heat for its casting, but it didn't affect them at the cash register, so the need to change wasn't nearly as big from a business sense as it was from a social pressure sense.

Unfortunately, new management did ultimately try to calm the inclusion crowd calling for their gorgeous heads. But when they bent the knee, they also bent the ratings, and after scaling back the show and broadening the casting pool, viewership fell every year from 2015 to 2018.

Yes, it would be right to point out that some of the decline comes from TV viewing habits changing, but nothing changes them faster than a successful show getting away from the formula viewers tuned in for. In that respect, you might argue that Victoria's Secret is the *Game of Thrones* of underwear, albeit with a smaller dwarf population.

Either way you slice it, the annual broadcast, which debuted with 12.4 million viewers, was down to 3.8 million by 2018, and the show that once broke the internet was officially broke, then canceled altogether.

The company's then CFO, Stuart Burgdoerfer, said the angels got sent off to that big runway in the sky because of sales figures, as there was no appreciable jump in the number of women shopping for Victoria's Secret products in the days after the show aired.

This is where appeasing the mob is so dangerous for companies. Yes, inclusion is fine and fabulous and everything else we need to say to not get our houses burned down by the tolerance crowd. But when you let the hive mind of the internet run your boardroom, you'll often see profits and viewership vanish, while none of the changes you implement actually change anything for anyone.

Even after the inclusion cops forced Victoria's Secret to ditch some of the traditional models, the truth is we're still not nearly as good-looking as the new lineup anyway.

Why?

Because they're *supermodels*.

They are exceptionally good-looking people who have God-given gifts that a lot of us don't. If anything, this new lineup makes you feel worse about yourself when you realize that even a size 20 is still twenty times hotter than you. In the Victoria's Secret heyday we all understood that we didn't need to compete with models or see them as evil agents sent here to demean us into killing ourselves to look like them.

If anything we needed to marvel at them, which is exactly what millions of men *and women* did. Does that mean other types of people aren't wildly attractive? Of course not. Nor does it mean women who don't look like these gals should feel lesser about themselves. Which is why, for my money, there are two lessons in this chapter worth taking with you.

For one, no woman or man should ever get too wrapped up in what happens in commercials, because nothing you see on TV is real.

Cereal commercials use *glue* to portray milk because it shines better on camera. Steaks get those fine-looking grill marks by using shoe polish to make the color more pronounced. Grapes are covered in spray-on deodorant to give them a matte look. Pancakes are covered with *motor oil* because the dough absorbs maple syrup too easily.

And, yes, models are oiled up and airbrushed down to make them look infinitely hotter so they can sell you a sexual fantasy. You shouldn't let it influence your behavior any more than you would any other commercials.

For instance, you never hear your doorbell ring and expect to see a talking gecko standing on the doormat, selling you car insurance. And if you do, it might be time to fix your carbon monoxide detector.

But perhaps the bigger lesson is that the last people on earth a lingerie company should *ever* be taking advice from is the outrage mob, because these people don't get laid.

Trust me, if they did, they wouldn't spend all day on the internet trying to ruin it for the rest of us.

Washington and Wilson

There was a time in this country when the biggest threat to a statue of George Washington was a pigeon. But that was before the cancel crowd started giving historical figures a different kind of bird.

In what has to be considered the dumbest cancel crusade of all time, George Washington, aka the Father of Our Country, became a target for removal at . . . *wait for it* . . . George Washington University.

Dude.

This is like canceling *Santa* at the North Pole. Except the people who tried to cancel Washington would never whack Santa because they're a bunch of children. And let's face it, if anybody can relate to a guy who comes only once a year, it's an angry Twitter troll with no profile picture.

It started in June 2022, when the board of trustees at GW University announced it was retiring the school's moniker, the Colonials, because students criticized it for glorifying colonialism, slavery, and discrimination. I guess no history professors were available to explain that George Washington fought against the colonizers.

Now, to be clear, the mascot wasn't enslaving anyone during the halftime show or taking away anyone's land. No, if you've watched George Washington's football team over the years, you'd know that their offense rarely gains *any* ground.

The removal was simply the end result of a review process that began at the height of the George Floyd riots in 2020, when the outrage mob had put a hit out on pretty much anything related to the founding of the country. The claim is that we were so systemically racist, we needed to erase anything related to our beginnings in order to get the problem under control.

They did mean *anything* related to our founding:

Just days after the mascot mania started, a student's op-ed sprang up in the *Washington Post*, of all places, calling on George Washington's complete cancellation from the school, given his ownership of slaves in the 1700s.

Yes, you read that right.

A student who chose to go to a school named after George Washington chose to publish an op-ed in a newspaper named after George Washington saying it was time to remove George Washington.

I've said it before in this book and I'll say it again: there has never been a dumber time to be alive.

Now, it goes without saying that the only reason these kids had a college to complain at and a country that puts up with it was because of guys like General George Washington, who won us our independence from England and created a place where their speech rights were protected. Same logic applies for the staff at the *Washington Post*.

Apparently, this was lost on them when they pressed "play" on a piece that claimed it was time to chop down Washington like a cherry tree because, quote:

> *Racism has always been a problem at GW. At the university's founding in 1821, enrollment was restricted to White men. In 1954, then-university president Cloyd Heck Marvin employed numerous efforts to preserve segregation, arguing for a "homogenous" group of White students.*

The author is correct in pointing out that racial attitudes were different in 1821, but everything the op-ed rails against in terms of segregation was overcome decades ago.

Let me say it one more time for those of you who slept through the earlier chapters, including my editor.

No country on earth has fought harder to create a level field for all races than America. There was an actual *war* that claimed over half a million lives in the name of ending slavery. Yes, and when that was done, we spent the next hundred-plus years fighting to integrate society. (A lot of European countries like to pat themselves on the back for this too. Countries that are 98 percent white.)

The bad news is that, yes, this country got started under a setup nobody would be okay with in modern times. The good news is we've made monumental racial progress that seemed nearly unimaginable in this country one hundred years ago. Even back in 1962, the producers of *The Jetsons* thought the future held a higher chance of *flying cars* than an interracial carpool. Fast-forward to today, and the only thing up in the sky are the gas prices and society is as integrated as it's ever been.

That doesn't mean we should stop striving to be better, but we do have to stop pretending that America has the same racial attitudes in 2024 as it did in 1824, because it's a profound insult to everyone who sacrificed so much to get us where we are. In the 1950s this country had separate lunch counters. Nowadays we don't have separate anything, although many people would support a constitutional amendment for separate dance floors, if only to protect white people's self-esteem.

Seriously, though, if you do cancel Washington—at Washington University no less—is everyone just supposed to walk around pretending the guy never existed? Or do the students who knowingly enrolled in a school named after George Washington now schedule time every week to pretend they were against him the whole time? There are no intelligent answers to these questions because the people canceling stuff aren't thinking in productive terms. They're cultural arsonists who set fires for the sole purpose of extinguishing them so they can be celebrated for their enlightenment.

There's no tangible improvement to anything in society by canceling an ex-president who's been dead over two hundred years. It doesn't boost test scores at failing schools. It doesn't help anyone get a job to pay off their massive student debt. It simply feeds an insatiable need for self-righteousness from left-wing activists who live to say they know better than everyone else.

George Washington was not a perfect man. I doubt one ever existed, outside of Burt Reynolds, of course. That's okay, as long as we are remembering our heroes *in spite of* the bad things rather than *for* the bad things.

It's not hard to find valid criticisms of the most revered people in modern times: Mother Teresa, Martin Luther King Jr., John F. Kennedy, Pope John Paul II, and so on. That doesn't mean we agree with everything they did. Franklin Delano Roosevelt put Japanese Americans into internment camps during World War II and they still named a highway after him in New York City. It was the least they could do, considering how much safer he made the roads.

They're just jokes, people! And we have the freedom to tell them because of past presidents like Roosevelt who led us through some of the darkest periods in our history.

And it goes without saying that none of them would have had a country to lead in the first place were it not for the courage George Washington showed in leading the revolt against the British. We were under absolutely tyrannical rule as a colony, and we would still be under it without Washington, which is no way to live.

I mean, sure, we'd all sound smarter if we had that British accent to put an intellectual coat of polish on every word that came out of our mouths. But Americans are not a people who can spend all their tax money pumping up a monarchy. And the food would be terrible.

Forget dealing with a British king. We couldn't even handle the ridiculousness of a British prince named Harry or his wife named Dipshit.

Ours is a country that can barely tolerate the Kansas City Royals, let alone the real ones. So for winning us our independence alone, George Washington's name should remain in good standing as long as there is an America.

Thankfully, as you read this, his name is still a thing at George Washington University. If anything, the board had the self-awareness to realize that even in this age of performative stupidity on steroids, removing Washington from *Washington* would be weapons-grade stupid.

You can't do it for the same reasons you can't remove Elvis from Graceland. One is synonymous with the other so deal with it and move on with your lives, because as a wise man once said, "We can't go on together / With suspicious minds."

Okay, I'll pump the brakes on the Elvis puns before somebody steps all over my blue suede shoes.

Of course, not every ex-president was able to keep his name on a college, and Woodrow Wilson would tell you as much if you owned a Ouija board.

Now if you asked most Americans, they'd tell you that "Wilson" was the volleyball Tom Hanks spoke to in *Cast Away*. We're honestly not the best at history. But, yes, there was another Wilson who was our twenty-eighth president, serving from 1913 to 1921.

Prior to landing the gig on LinkedIn, he had a long and storied history with Princeton University. He obtained an undergraduate degree in 1879 and returned in 1890 as a professor, teaching twelve years on campus before becoming the university's president in 1902.

It's also worth noting that as a student he set the campus record for keg stands in one semester, posting a very impressive fifty-one in the fall of 1878.

It's *also* worth noting that I'm making the keg stand story up completely. But he did oppose Prohibition, so you can read into that whatever you want.

President Wilson died in 1924, three years after he left office. But his name was still held in the highest regard nearly two and a half decades after his death. That's more than you'll be able to say for you and me, thanks to our old social media posts.

In 1948, Princeton announced it was adding a graduate program and applied Wilson's name to its School of Public and International Affairs.

Just so we're clear, nobody names a college after someone who's in trouble with society at the time. If you don't believe me, ask my ex-girlfriend Ghislaine.

That was a Jeffrey Epstein joke for those of you who might have missed it. I'm aware the dude was a creep and dirtbag. Although the Clintons always said he was a great hang.

The point is Wilson had been dead for twenty-four years when Princeton chose the name, so you'd assume this was settled law. It certainly appeared that way for the next sixty-five years, as his name remained on the school without incident.

It wasn't until 2015, when battles had broken out over old statues across the country, that the cancel crowd started scrutinizing ex-presidents too. As kids were getting clicks on social media for tearing down Christopher Columbus statues and anything to do with the Confederacy, a group of student protesters at Princeton took it a step further and went in on the names of buildings.

Apparently, they didn't have any obvious statues to tear down, and they were feeling left out, so in the fall of 2015 they sent a petition around campus demanding that the school take Wilson's name off its buildings because of his past support for segregation.

To bring attention to their cause, they also occupied the school president's office for a sit-in. Photos of the event show that, like all people engaged in a pivotal fight for equality, they brought their laptops so they could multitask.

What do we want? The Wi-Fi password! When do we want it? Now!

The restful unrest grew loud enough on campus that the board of trustees formed a special committee to review concerns over Wilson's legacy. That 2015 probe lasted several months but ultimately ended with the board recommending the school keep Wilson's name despite the fact that "his values were not always consistent with those of the students or the faculty."

There were no counterprotests at this point because the board had wisely stretched things well beyond the week of rage on campus and waited till the kids were done with the cause to announce the results.

In June 2020, during the same societal purge that tried to whack Washington, Princeton students went back in on the quest to make Woodrow take a walk. The climate was much different than in 2015 because we were in the midst of the George Floyd protests and the cancel crowd was calling for the removal of pretty much any government figure who wasn't running on the Democratic ticket that summer.

It wasn't the type of thing they could let die down because, unlike a 2015 protest, the cultural purge of 2020 was not confined to their campus. It was countrywide in everything we did.

Statues, syrup mascots, shows on TV—everything was in play, as long as you could attack it from your phone and it wouldn't help anyone in real life.

If you didn't give the mob what it wanted, the entirety of social media was poised to call your institution racist for the better part of eternity. Faced with this reality, Princeton's board of trustees folded faster than Arnold Schwarzenegger's maid on date night.

Less than a week after the uproar began, and less than five years after the school had stood by Wilson's name, the board released a letter saying our twenty-eighth president was now a goner. The school cited his support for "racist thinking and policies," a decision that was made more urgent by the high-profile police killings around the country that summer.

Translation: We know we spent years exploring this very idea and didn't agree with it, but that was before our donors cared. And just like that, nearly seventy-five years after it was painted on, Wilson's name was washed right off.

What's funny about this one is that while the mob was rejoicing, the board quietly announced that Wilson's name was going to remain on the prestigious alumni award given in his honor each year. The school justified the decision by saying it was endowed by a financial gift that came with "a legal obligation to name the prize for Wilson." Which is a *very* fancy way of saying the school didn't want to give that money back to whoever forked it over.

There was no backlash for keeping the cash because by then the mob had got its way and moved on, saving countless someones from experiencing something terrible or whatever. It was never really made clear what this would accomplish.

In the summer of 2020, getting something canceled became a status symbol, sort of like going to Coachella. Saying you did it was supposed to mean something to everybody else, although nobody ever had anything to show for it. Aside from the STD, in Coachella's case.

Woodrow Wilson wasn't the most objectionable person commemorated in America; he was just the most objectionable person Princeton students could find once they needed one. Nothing changed in the country by removing Wilson's name other than the amount of digital dopamine the protesters shot up on social media for getting those cancel points. The school loved it because Wilson's cancellation was a *yuge* win-win for them. The board was able to silence the outrage crowd by creating the appearance that they held the same values. And while everybody was high-fiving in the student center because that racist relic had gone away, the board got right back to investing those sweet, sweet endowment checks that were sent in his name.

You see, for all of their posturing about principles, colleges are just a business. And if placating the outrage mob is good for their bottom line, they'll get behind just about any uprising that happens on campus. Which is why it took so many schools as long as it did to condemn student groups who supported the attacks against Israel by Hamas terrorists. It wasn't the board's morals that finally got them to pipe up, it was their donors in the case of Harvard and UPenn.

Think about the Biden administration's push for student loan forgiveness. If you notice, *not one college* came out against it despite the fact that schools are the ones who are owed all of the money that would be "forgiven."

Why?

Because they're still getting paid, in full.

Yes, the students who took the loans out would be off the hook, but the cost would be passed along to the taxpayers, who didn't sign on for any of this. Incredibly the Biden administration claimed to be passing around the debt in the name of fairness, which is like passing around a bottle of tequila in the name of sobriety.

Thankfully, the Supreme Court struck down the program in June 2023, but even if the Biden administration wins its appeals someday, the colleges aren't worried one bit because none of this tackles the real cause of all this debt, which is the runaway cost of a degree. In fact, if the government is going to pick up the tab, why not keep raising the cost?

Student loan forgiveness was a license to drive the tuition costs to the moon. They don't care who sends that monthly check, whether it's students or taxpayers. Even if the cash comes from a bunch of Woodrow Wilson supporters, a man they now claim is a racist piece of garbage even though his name was on their buildings, like, a half hour ago.

That's the fraud behind most cancels. The people who give out the cancels—often colleges and corporations—aren't actually agreeing with the position of the protesters so much as they're just trying to make them go away.

Trust me, if Princeton thought Woodrow Wilson was the devil, he wouldn't have spent seventy years on the side of the library. And if student protesters thought he was evil incarnate, they wouldn't have enrolled in a school with his name on it.

If someone opened an Adolf Hitler University, it wouldn't take seventy years before people decided to take his name off the library. Because our opinion on Hitler was settled law for as long as he's lived. That's not the case with a guy like Woodrow Wilson, whose views were mainstream enough in his lifetime to get him elected president twice. And remember, they weren't commemorating how much he liked *Birth of a Nation*. They were commemorating his role in the birth of the United Nations.

Under the eyes of his contemporaries, Wilson's biggest offense would be the fact that he didn't own a time machine that could show him just how much society evolved in the decades after he helped us win World War I.

Universities play along with the mob rule format not because they agree with their beliefs but because it's good for business. Believe me, college deans are smart enough to know the universal truths that biological men can't have a baby and that biological women can't pick out a good movie.

They'll espouse whatever beliefs keep them on the right side of that week's outrage movement because colleges are just fancy hookers who turn whatever trick they gotta to get that tuition. They'll charge you for a degree that has absolutely no commensurate job to go with it. They'll push you decades into debt at a time in your life when you still don't have a full vision of what you want to do with it. They'll call a dead president a racist while pocketing all kinds of dead presidents that were sent in his name.

It's rough out there on them campus streets. And it's only gonna get worse if Democrats ever win their student loan forgiveness battle because doing so will let colleges drive the prices up even higher.

As the father of a teenage son, you'd think I'd be concerned about the rising cost of college, but the truth is I'm not worried at all.

My son is six foot five. He's getting a women's basketball scholarship.

XXX

You might think the adult film industry would be immune to cancel culture, but even they've been forced to pull out from time to time.

Here we go!

Now, to be clear, the people we'll profile in this chapter did not get canceled from adult films. Because, let's face it, if that industry gives you a bad grade, there's always something you can do for the professor to change it.

In this instance the problems began when those sexy stepmoms left home and started interacting with the rest of America's youth, as actress Brandi Love attempted to do. In July 2021, Love tweeted a screenshot of an email showing she'd been banned from Turning Point USA's student summit in Florida.

To be clear, she attempted to portray this as an outright cancel—as if she had done something offensive. But in this instance, it wasn't quite what she had done—or who she had done—so much as how many people saw it happen. You see, Turning Point has a stated policy of not allowing adult performers at its events because they're attended by minors.

I don't doubt there were plenty of participants who were disappointed to learn they wouldn't be able to rub elbows, and other things, with the XXX legend, but the rules are the rules. Although I must say, if Turning Point is really going to push family values as hard as it does, it seems a little crazy to ban the star of *Mother Daughter Exchange Club 24*.

Yes, they really did make twenty-four editions of *Mother Daughter Exchange Club*. No, you don't need to see the first twenty-three to understand the twenty-fourth. I'm only pointing it out because I wish somebody told me before I spent a whole weekend researching this chapter. That poor family waiting behind me to use the computer at the public library . . .

Anyway. While Love wasn't canceled from her job per se, the stigma surrounding her industry has troubled so many porn stars who attempted to move into other careers. Some lost their gigs, while others were able to get off. Unfortunately, they still got fired afterward.

One of them was actress Lonna Wells, who claims she was canned from Taco Bell after taking a job when the pandemic shut down her film shoots. Now, if we're being honest, there are worse things to catch on a porn set than Covid, but the industry wasn't chancing it, mainly because none of the guys wearing lab coats were real doctors. Not saying I'm an expert on the issue, but experience has taught me never to trust a medical professional who takes your temperature with his finger.

Wells told the Daily Beast she was completely up-front with the manager at the Arkansas Taco Bell and was assured she could work the drive-thru no matter how many miles she had on her chassis. However, less than a week later, Wells was fired.

To hear her tell it, she got a call at 7:30 a.m. telling her she was canned because a "God-fearing Christian" complained that they didn't feel comfortable giving the restaurant any business because there was a woman working the drive-thru who starred in dirty movies.

I'd just like to point out that if this is true, and they really did fire her after *one customer* complained, this person had to be fat as *hell* for their business to matter that much. Seriously, whoever it was didn't fear God half as much as the treadmill.

Now the company claims Wells was whacked because she violated "policies and procedures," so it's tough to tell who's giving us the straight dope here.

Although, if Taco Bell did fire her because she worked in porn, it's a bit hypocritical, given how many people their food has screwed over the years.

Knock. Knock. Knock.

"Hurry up in there!"

The good news is, a few years after the firing, Wells appears to be back on her feet. And her counter. And her kitchen table.

Resa Woodward is another former porn star; she performed under the name Robyn Foster. So far as I know, she never applied to work at a Taco Bell. She did, however, land a teaching gig at an all-girls school in Texas. Unfortunately, she, too, was fired after district officials learned of her previous work in porn.

Woodward worked in education for fifteen years, starting out in North Carolina and then Florida before moving on to Dallas. In January 2017 she was teaching sixth-grade science at the Balch Springs Middle School when she got pulled out of her classroom by district officials who'd received an anonymous tip about her previous career.

The firing came quickly, with the *Dallas Morning News* summarizing it as such:

> *According to Woodward's termination letter, obtained this week, district officials fired her because her previous work "in adult content media" was accessible on the internet and available to the public. That "casts the District in a negative light and adversely affects the District."*

Let the record show that Resa Woodward was the first person to get fired because someone else forgot to delete their search history.

Where's the justice?

Woodward appealed her firing to the board, claiming she was forced into the industry by a controlling man when she was younger. She also pointed out in her appeals letter that she'd earned the highest rating of "exemplary" in the school's distinguished-teacher program. She was also a current nominee for District Teacher of the Year and had also been nominated for Campus Teacher of the Year in 2016–17.

Meaning this might be a sticky issue, in more ways than one, but she was clearly a woman who got the job done.

Sadly, Woodward was not granted an appeal hearing by the Texas Education Agency and did wind up losing her job in the end. She has since found other work, but I can't help but think her firing was a major loss for that school district. I mean, if anything could finally get dads to show up to parent-teacher conferences, this was it.

Of course, it's not just female porn stars who've gotten the shaft from their employers. A Roman college professor was fired after his previous work as a gay porn actor surfaced. Because everyone knows if you wanna do gay stuff in Rome, you work at the Vatican.

Don't you *dare* judge me for that joke.

They did it, not me.

Ruggero Freddi was an Italian man who moved to America to work in the adult film industry under the name Carlo Masi. He starred in films such as *Big N' Plenty* and *Man Country*.

I'm not gonna spoil the plot of *Man Country*, but I will give the director credit because it took a lot of balls to make this film.

Freddi retired from porn in 2009 at the age of thirty-four and obtained degrees in engineering and mathematics, where he was a natural at adding to 69.

In 2017 he returned to his home country and became an engineering professor at Sapienza University. Things seemed to be going well until he posted a shirtless picture of himself online, at which point someone recognized him and notified the school. Freddi was fired almost immediately, but dig this: he filed a lawsuit in an Italian court claiming he was unfairly dismissed and he actually won the case!

It was a bittersweet moment because he was hoping for a hung jury.

Rim shots aside, at long last, I just want to say that porn actors have been stigmatized throughout history, but I think their new employers should stop giving them a hard time. The tales of abuse and addiction that plague their industry are legendary, and anyone who truly wants to make good on a new life should have every chance at pursuing one.

Sure, their acting isn't the best, and, yes, the absurdly fake plotlines are thinner than Jesse Watters's real hair. But employers in every industry would be right to hire them, because, after all, this is a crowd that can handle any position.

Ye

Kanye West rose to fame in the early 2000s as a mega-talented rapper and producer. He had an alter ego named Yeezus, whom he deemed to be the Black Jesus, although historians will note some subtle differences between the two figures. Mainly the fact that Yeezus was known to turn water into weed. And you wouldn't expect to find twelve Apostles in his dressing room, although twelve strippers was *never* outta the question.

Unfortunately, Yeezus gave one too many controversial sermons, and his career had a Last Supper of its own in 2022. No cancel has gotten any uglier any faster than Kanye's. But seeing as it involved some praise of Adolf Hitler, we shouldn't be surprised his career went down in a *heil* of bullets.

That joke was for the grammar folks.

Long before the cancel crowd called him collect, West had a storied history of doing outrageous things to get attention. He stormed the stage at the 2009 MTV Video Music Awards, interrupting Taylor Swift before she could accept the Moonman statue for Best Video by a Female Artist. Swift had just leaned in to begin her speech when West grabbed the mic and shouted, "I'mma let you finish, but Beyoncé had one of the best music videos of all time!"

Like Taylor, the crowd was absolutely stunned. Although, when it comes to bad behavior at awards shows, I'd put it at a 6 on a scale of 1 to Will Smith.

Yeezus made *major* headlines for the VMA stunt, just the same as he did in 2005 when he trashed President Bush during a live telethon for Hurricane Katrina victims.

West was making a presentation with *Austin Powers* star Mike Myers when he went off script and accused the president of being Dr. Evil, saying, "George Bush doesn't care about Black people." It was the tail end of a two-minute rant, and the second he said it, producers immediately cut away to the next presenter, *Friday* star Chris Tucker. He clearly wasn't expecting it to go down this way, and you could tell because he had the troubled look of a stoned teenager who unexpectedly runs into his parents.

KID: "Mom and Dad? What are you guys doing here?"
PARENTS: "We *live* here, honey."
KID: "*Duh!*" (He laughs nervously, wondering in his head if they knew he was stoned.)
PRO TIP: Yes, your parents *always* knew you were stoned.

It's unclear if Kanye was puffing the Devil's Lettuce the night he bashed Bush. But we do know his ridiculous comments exploded all over the media. This, of course, happened the very same week his new album, *Late Registration*, came out in stores, which I'm sure is a *total* coincidence, wink, wink, nudge, nudge.

West caught hell in the press but Black Jesus's album rose from the ashes, racking up an impressive 3.5 million sales. It also went on to win him a Grammy for Best Rap Solo Performance for the song "Gold Digger."

It was his second Grammy in a row, following the previous year's win for "Jesus Walks," a song he promoted to great controversy when Yeezus himself appeared on the cover of *Rolling Stone* in a crown of thorns.

Kanye has always been rewarded for ridiculous behavior, but a lot of that had to do with his ridiculous talent. He was easily one of the greatest rappers of his generation, and prior to finding success on the microphone he had it in the mixing booth, producing hit songs for hip-hop megastars such as Jay-Z, Alicia Keys, Janet Jackson, and Jermaine Dupri. There was also a fashion line and a sneaker brand with a price tag that was through the roof of the church. Therein lies another difference between our historical figures. Whereas Jesus washed poor people's feet, Yeezus made people poor by putting shoes on their feet.

Which is to say that while his charity work may not have been biblical, nobody questioned Yeezus's ability. However, his penchant for publicity stunts and hour-long rants left many people questioning his sanity, and it turns out where there was weed smoke, there was fire.

In June 2018, he admitted to having actual mental health issues on his album *Ye*, which was now his newer, shorter nickname for himself.

The album was loaded with dark lyrics about suicide, premeditated murder, and, yes, his bipolar disorder. Now, most people assumed he was nuts the second he married into the Kardashian family, but this was his first acknowledgment of a medical condition.

During the promotional tour, he opened up to radio host Charlamagne Tha God about his previous hospitalization for a mental breakdown as well as his ongoing struggles with opioid addiction. Normally, showing this sort of vulnerability would garner sympathy for a public figure. In West's case there wasn't any, because he came out as bipolar the exact same week he came out as a Donald Trump supporter, tweeting:

> *You don't have to agree with Trump but the mob can't make me not love him. We are both dragon energy. He is my brother.*

In the interest of full disclosure, we're yet to get the 23andMe DNA results back on the Kanye-Trump kinship. But I can confirm that this was the most unforgivable thing you could do in the entertainment industry at the time. Imagine the hate you'd get from wearing a Yankees jersey to a wedding reception in the South End of Boston, except the crowd was good-looking.

Just when you thought Hollywood couldn't detest this dude more, West took that dragon energy to the White House in October 2018 wearing a bright red MAGA hat.

The media absolutely lost their *shit* when Kanye began by kneeling at the *Resolute* Desk. Although I'm not entirely sure why. I mean, it's not like he's the first person to take a knee in front of the president. And if you don't believe me, ask Monica Lewinsky.

West quickly declared his love for Trump and went on to tell reporters, "You're tasting a fine wine with this guy," in reference to the president. He also encouraged the haters to stop mocking Trump, saying, "If he looks bad, we look bad."

He then unlocked his phone on camera, showing us all that the password was "000000." There's a joke to be made about wanting easy access and marrying Kim Kardashian, but I'll tell it a few paragraphs from now.

It was a rambling mess of a meeting, although Trump appeared to enjoy the rare show of celebrity support. Kanye seemed thrilled to be in the center ring of the biggest media circus the world has ever known.

But unlike his wife's visit to the White House the previous spring, the entertainment industry was not as forgiving toward Kanye. Kim had shown up to make an impassioned plea for prison reform, and people seemed to respect her commitment to the issue. After all, this was a woman who's gotten *a lot* of guys off over the years. (Promises made, promises kept.)

Kanye seemed to be chasing attention in his usual defy-the-conventional-crowd kind of way, but people weren't having it anymore.

Things got worse in 2020 when he made his own run for the White House, which left onlookers wondering if this was a serious issue or just a guy with serious issues. We figured that one out at his very first rally, when the future president broke down crying in South Carolina during a wild rant about abortion. It was another moment that might have garnered him sympathy, but once again he topped it off by throwing a wild pitch, saying, "Harriet Tubman never actually freed the slaves. She just had the slaves go work for other white people."

Dude.

Nobody has ever copied off me on a history test, but even I know that "circle wouldn't get the square" if this was his answer on a *Hollywood Squares* reboot.

Ye had quickly become an outcast in the court of public opinion, and as his presidential run fizzled, so did his marriage to Kim. Sources had told TMZ she was incredibly bothered by the White House bid, and I'm sure it didn't help that Kanye began taking shots at her family on Twitter, referring to the matriarch Kris Jenner as "Kris Jong Un." Which of course is a totally unfair comparison because Kris Jenner has never been accused of feeding family members to a pack of dogs. If she did that, she wouldn't have any sex tapes to leak. Plus, most of the Kardashian pets go missing before they can get around to eating anyone.

Sad but true story, although you've gotta laugh knowing they're the only missing-dog posters with airbrushed photos.

Back to the humans in the family. Kim spoke openly about the many attempts to get Ye help, but she ultimately ended up filing for divorce in January 2021. The couple had been married nearly seven years, which is actually forty-two years in Hollywood because you count celebrity relationships the way you count cat years. Although not all the celebrities use the litter box when they're upset at their spouse, but enough about Amber Heard.

On the plus side, the split between Kim and Kanye appeared to be amicable, with the reality TV legend asking for joint custody of their kids. At the advice of Kris Jenner, she even offered to split the house, with Kim getting the inside and Kanye getting the outside.

It was a rough couple of months for the man now known as Ye. But while the celebrity marriage may have been gone, he still had a thriving career in rap and fashion despite all the bipolar disorder and presidential pandemonium. Not only was he a billionaire, thanks to his partnerships with Adidas, Gap, and Balenciaga, but he was also the subject of an upcoming documentary by the MRC film/TV studio. In addition, he'd just taped an episode of LeBron James's HBO series *The Shop*, which was set to air in October 2022.

All of that changed when West once again courted controversy by sporting a "White Lives Matter" T-shirt at his Paris Fashion Week show.

It was yet another move straight out of his no-publicity-is-bad-publicity playbook. But the media fallout was definitely different this time because he was taking a shot at the patron saint of corporate virtue signaling, the Black Lives Matter movement. And this was *before* most people realized the leaders of that organization had blown big bucks on mansions and gifts for their families.

Kanye was absolutely clobbered in the press, and he responded on Twitter, saying:

Everyone knows that Black Lives Matter was a scam. Now it's over. You're welcome.

He went on to add:

Here's my latest response when people ask me why I made a tee that says white lives matter . . . THEY DO.

In a normal world, he wouldn't be ruined for simply sharing a controversial opinion, but these are not normal times. The social pressure on celebrities to play along with the conventional wisdom of the left is incalculably huge. Mainly because the people shoving diversity and equity down our throats do not really support either one.

The holy water was beginning to boil when Yeezus went on a late-night Twitter rant that didn't exactly lower the temperature. At the time of the post, Instagram had just placed restrictions on his account for making a series of bizarre statements. It's worth noting that Instagram is owned by Meta, which is led by Mark Zuckerberg, who happens to be Jewish. This fact was not lost on Ye when he responded to the restrictions. Before we see his reaction, I want you to take a second to focus, because the tweet you're about to read cost over *one billion dollars.*

I'm a bit sleepy tonight but when I wake up I'm going death con 3 On JEWISH PEOPLE. The funny thing is I actually can't be Anti Semitic because black people are actually Jew also You guys have toyed with me and tried to black ball anyone whoever opposes your agenda.

Weird. Out there. And never a good idea to threaten DEFCON 3 on any group of people—or anyone, for that matter—but we weren't done.

Ye also posted an image that portrayed a swastika inside the Star of David. Because why alienate 99.9 percent of society when you can alienate 100 percent? By the time he woke up, Twitter and Instagram had gone DEFCON 3 on him, suspending his accounts, denouncing his behavior, and touching off one of the quickest cancels the world will ever witness.

We can debate free speech rights all we want, and there's clearly a strong history of this guy saying stupid shit for attention. But I'm telling you for your own sake, nowhere in the world is there a man who'd be better off in his career if only he spent more time threatening Jewish people on Twitter. Well, maybe in parts of the Middle East. And a chunk of eastern Europe. Even some parts of Africa. Anyway, he lives in America, and, contrary to what they might tell you at an Ivy League college, America is a bad place for a corporate pitchman to threaten all Jews on Twitter.

Now, Ye could very well have been joking, but when there are billion-dollar branding partnerships on the table, the Holocaust is never going to work as a punch line. And given the fact that he'd already upset the BLM applecart, what started out as a cancel pebble rolled into a boulder at warp speed.

Within two hours of the post, West had been trashed on Twitter by some of the most respected minds in Hollywood, and also Gwyneth Paltrow. The corporate world took it from there, with Gap and Balenciaga immediately severing ties with him the following morning. This, of course, led the way for Adidas to drop out later that week. Losing his fashion line caused Ye to fall off the Forbes billionaire list, and it also sent his partnership with T.J.Maxx off to that big clearance rack in the sky. On the entertainment side, MRC scrapped its upcoming documentary, and LeBron's agents announced they would not be airing the already recorded episode of *The Shop*. You know you've gone off the rails when a guy who played with a flat-earther named Kyrie Irving thinks your views aren't well-rounded enough.

To his credit, Kyrie apologized for his flat-earth phase a long time ago, but, sadly, Ye refused to quit while he was behind and did a series of truly bizarre interviews in a futile effort to defend his remarks. The sequence of strikeouts culminated with a fully masked West offering praise for Adolf Hitler on Alex Jones's show, saying, "I see some good things in Hitler."

This statement was historic for multiple reasons. Not only did it officially destroy one of the greatest rap careers in the world, but it will also go down as perhaps the only time in history that Alex Jones was the most *sane person* on a TV set. I'm pretty sure Ye was trying to make a larger point but, speaking to you as a guy who gives speeches for a living, I promise, if you've already lost the crowd, it's pretty hard to win them back with *Nazis*.

To that point, his agency, CAA, fired him, and even Peloton took his music off all of its playlists. Turns out Kanye was prophetic when he sang "All Falls Down," because it definitely did.

Now, I'm an old-school kind of dude in that I don't think you should judge anyone until you walk a mile in their shoes. But it's impossible in this instance because no stores carry them anymore.

What I will say is that Ye is a dude who clearly suffers from mental illness, and on one level I can always offer grace to people who've seemingly lost their way in life. Think of how many vegans I've had on my radio show. These people clearly ain't right in the head, but I don't want to outright ruin them.

That being said, I unequivocally support the companies who exercised their right to cancel Ye. Some people tried to frame it as an attack on his speech rights, but the truth is the First Amendment wasn't violated here in any way. Nowhere in the Constitution does it say that companies can't *fire a spokesperson* for expressing wildly controversial views that they don't agree with.

The First Amendment is there to let us protest, criticize, and call out our government without being imprisoned. Ye has not been jailed for his comments. He's simply been sentenced to commercial death.

Yeah, the bad news for Yeezus is that his commercial career would appear to be completely dead. The good news is if he really is the Black Jesus, he'll be making a comeback any day now.

Zoo Worker

I was going to begin by welcoming everyone to the final chapter of the book, but then it dawned on me that, for most readers, the party ended at least a hundred pages ago. That being said, the fact that *you* stuck around means a lot, so *thanks*, pal. My writing career would be nothing without the fine folks like yourself who enjoy reading at a third-grade level. Thanks to you, I now enjoy the privilege of calling myself an author, at least until the reviews come out.

Our final cancel has much in common with the others, mainly the fact that it changed absolutely nothing in society for the better. And it goes without saying that 99 percent of the people who forced it have no recollection of these events, because once the mob got its way, their stampede of self-righteousness raged on to another social media battlefield.

It's a hit-and-run strategy that can whack a career in hours, but it's also the reason why most of their victims were ultimately able to make a comeback. You see, cancels succeed only when the mob can amplify outrage at speeds that horrify corporations into acting. Yes, our new and constantly connected life on social media means we're all one bad hashtag away from unemployment. No, you won't be gone forever.

And the weird part is nobody who wanted you fired will even care when you come back, because, truth be told, they didn't care about the cause you were canceled for to begin with.

How many people who led the charge to get Gilbert Gottfried fired for tweeting about the Japanese tsunami flew over to Tokyo afterward to help out the victims of his jokes? I'm guessing zero, mainly because there weren't any. Do you think *anyone* who was floating to safety on what used to be the roof of their house was logging on to American Twitter to see what people were saying about their situation? Of course not. Sadly, if they were using their iPhone for anything, it was an oar.

Which is all it's good for in this country if you have T-Mobile, like me. I don't want to get sidetracked with a talk about lousy wireless carriers, but, dude, my T-Mobile phone loses service *in* the T-Mobile store! At the moment we're trying to upgrade to a Styrofoam cup and a string, but we're waiting to see if our plan qualifies. Okay, with that venting session out of the way, let's move forward, with one bar of service if we're lucky.

I know there are people reading this who think we shouldn't joke about tragedies, but the truth is *you* shouldn't if it's not right for you. There are millions of us who use comedy as a coping mechanism. We're the ones who laugh when the world makes us feel like strapping a bomb to our chest and sprinting off a cliff. Please don't be scared by the darkness of that analogy if you're someone who cares about me. I've gained so much weight writing this book there's *no way* the strap is gonna fit around my body. Even so, nobody should be able to deny anyone their way of grieving.

It's not just jokes, though. People try to limit speech rights everywhere in this day and age. We've seen them do it with vaccines, elections, biology, you name it. It's an exercise in weaponized censorship that is everywhere in liberal politics, where they push the absurd notion that "speech is violence" to get their way.

Agree with our policies or people will die!

It's completely ridiculous, but it's tragically reshaped society in a way that's left us more focused on words instead of deeds. Think about it. An individual criminal rarely faces the collective backlash for assaulting someone that a comedian does for making fun of something in unacceptable terms.

Hell, Jeremy Meeks, aka the Hot Felon, had a violent arrest record long enough to wrap around the internet twice and he became a *supermodel* after his mug shot went viral. I'm happy for his success, but don't you think it's a little weird that some of the very same Fashion Weeks who dropped Kanye West for saying stupid shit also *hired* Jeremy Meeks after he assaulted a minor? I'm telling you our compass is broken from all this speech policing. And every time we lock up the language, it takes us further in the opposite direction of real solutions.

Sadly, it's not just happening to comedians and rappers, nor is this newfound obsession with words confined to just America. Did you know that over in London you're not even allowed to call someone a *pussy* anymore?

You have to call them "Prince Harry."

None of us benefit from living in a world of pretend purity, where the only people held in good standing are the folks who've never been on the wrong side of the angry keyboard crowd. Trust me, you don't want a social credit score to determine just how much freedom you have in life. If you do, move to Communist China. Or get married, whatever's easier.

The point I was trying to make before I got kicked out of my house was that, yes, a few of the people in this book should have *absolutely* gotten canceled for their behavior. I'm not gonna name names, but it rhymes with R. Kelly. I'd call out Bill Cosby, too, but he's not reading this because he has sight issues. If he could see, he'd probably be watching his favorite rom-com, *Sleeping Beauty*.

Don't you dare "too soon" me on that one. If this world is ever going to have a shot at being normal again, we need to save our digital fire for the dirtbags who *do* the bad stuff and not the folks who mock them for doing it.

Repeat after me: People who break the law in major ways deserve all of our societal scorn. But we shouldn't light the world on fire every time someone tells a tasteless joke or tweets something stupid after smoking enough weed to sedate a manatee. Of course, you don't have to *like* everything you hear, and nobody expects you to. But rather than letting the words of a stranger consume you with rage, allow me to suggest an old medical remedy we used to great success in the '80s and '90s:

It's called *chill the fuck out*.

Thankfully, as we wrap up this literary masterpiece, the mob is losing its leverage, because the average person is sick of living on the perpetual eve of destruction. And I'm encouraged that companies like Netflix are starting to realize it can't help the bottom line to reconfigure the entire business model every time an employee gets upset watching videos on the potty in the break room.

Every day more people are becoming hip to the fact that the cancel crowd's production model of burning it all down, just because, is truly unsustainable. And while we're not all the way out of the woods yet, once we do get past our newfound fixation on words, this scourge we called "cancel culture" will fall faster than cruise prices did after the *Titanic*.

Okay, that was a C-plus analogy *at best*. In my defense, I was going to make a joke about that submarine that imploded near the *Titanic*, but I couldn't put all the pieces together.

I don't know if Rochelle Robinson has ever attempted to visit the "Ship That God Couldn't Sink." (Spoiler alert: He could.) But history will show that she sank her own career at Chicago's Brookfield Zoo after hitting an iceberg on social media.

This one happened on Facebook in June 2015, at a time when you'd expect the people of Chicago to be in a much better mood. The Supreme Court had just upheld the Affordable Care Act, delivering a major win to President Obama, who hailed from the Hyde Park neighborhood. Over in the NHL, the hometown Blackhawks won the Stanley Cup. Even if you were a Chicagoan who didn't watch hockey, you could still be happy there was a ticker tape parade to drown out the sound of the gunfire for one day.

Chicago is a mess, which is all the more reason to get away to the Brookfield Zoo and marvel at the awesome animals. Unfortunately, not all the visitors knew how to behave, and nobody knows that better than the star of this chapter.

On June 8, 2015, Rochelle Robinson was in the middle of her shift when she took a time-out to post a selfie. The pic looked great, but she was about to find out that, like this book, her caption needed a better editor. Love you, Eric.

Okay, here's her post:

Wassup yall. At work serving these rude ass white people.

As a white people myself, I found her comment kind of hilarious, because I've seen plenty of rude-ass people of all colors at the zoo, and I don't doubt the staff is sick of dealing with them. The problem was she made a generalization about one race at a time when it was still considered frowned upon to single out any of them, including those evil, terrible, no-good whites. She would've been fine if she'd waited five years, until the year 2020, when the woke left made it fashionable to claim that all white people are inherently racist whether they realize it or not. Calling us rude would mean *nothing* when critical race theory is teaching white schoolchildren that they're literally oppressing their Black classmates. I mean, what's ruder than oppression?

The good news for Rochelle Robinson was that she achieved her goal of going viral on Facebook. The bad news was unemployment. Within hours of her post, users had shared it so much, it began to pop up on Twitter and Instagram, and with that, her job disappeared faster than the slow kid who climbs into the lion enclosure.

The zoo announced her firing in a Facebook statement that read as follows:

> *Yesterday, we became aware of the actions of a single employee which we agree are unacceptable. This employee's statements on social media are in violation of our policies and do not reflect our institution's values. We have zero tolerance for these kinds of divisive behaviors. We treat all employment matters confidentially but please know that we took prompt action to remedy the situation this morning. We hope you continue to hold Brookfield Zoo in high regard and not let the actions of one individual overshadow the longstanding good work of the Chicago Zoological Society.*

Luckily for the zoo, people did not hold it against them, and business continued to boom. But I can tell you firsthand that canceling Rochelle Robinson did nothing to get those rude-ass white people under control at our nation's zoos.

In the summer of 2023, I was at the incredible St. Louis Zoo with Jenny and Lincoln when a pudgy white toddler became an absolute legend in our family because of just how much of a monster he was being. Every time we ran into this family at a new exhibit, the kid was in the process of issuing another profanity-laced Yelp review, and for some reason it was hysterical. I understand you may not see the humor in a barbaric baby because you were raised right, but I promise, you have not lived until you've heard a three-year-old say, "That giraffe sucks! Fuck this zoo!"

For its part, the giraffe seemed unfazed by the criticism, as did the elephants and the antelopes. But I don't doubt the human staff had issues with the cursing kid. Just the same as the Chicago zoo worker probably had good reasons for being fed up with the white man. But it's important to understand that her motivation was not to attack white people. It was to look like she'd been attacked *by them*.

Social media rewards this sort of thing, so in her mind, it was a chance to go viral after she'd gone on break. That is the allure of playing this hot new game show, *Wheel of Victimhood*. Trashing someone who does you wrong will often win you cash and prizes. But be warned that sometimes you spin the wheel and bankrupt yourself instead.

This gal was trapped at work, feeling lousy, and tried to get high on digital dopamine by framing herself as the recipient of racial rudeness. And the crazy part is if she had posted a video of these "rude ass white people" giving her a hard time, her plan would've worked. Not only would they have been the ones doxed and fired, but she would've likely become a sympathetic figure online, which could've led to someone starting a GoFundMe account or, at the very least, the zoo giving her a promotion to signify that they were not on board with racism. Unfortunately, she worded her post wrong, and the zoo forced her to exit through the gift shop instead.

Which just goes to show you that nobody wins in a world that champions victimhood. But the fact that we've spent the last ten years doing it has taught way too many people to look for things to get offended by instead of living their lives in search of joy.

There was a time when the *only* reason people went to a comedy club was to laugh. Okay, some went to feel better about their life choices after seeing how damaged those of us who entered showbiz are. But laughing at jokes was the main attraction, whereas today you'll have people showing up to get attention for calling a joke out as offensive.

You can always see it coming when the light of a cell phone camera comes on during your set. This is why pretty much every club you go to now bans videos. They know the people who enjoy jokes sit back and laugh.

While the people who weaponize jokes sit up and film.

Who knows? Maybe you'll open the ol' inter-web someday to read a story about me getting canceled. Lord knows, I say enough crazy shit to pull it off. Sometimes I wonder if I'm doing it subconsciously, as if the former cabdriver in me really misses the smell of drugs and hookers. But that can't be it because I'm around congressmen all the time.

Regardless, if the Humor Patrol ever does lock me up and throw away the keyboard, please know that, like 99 percent of the people in this book, I didn't open my mouth in search of a problem. I opened it looking for a laugh. Because in the end we are all in the "fun business" on this earth. No matter what it says on your business card, if you die tomorrow, you're quickly going to realize that the whole point of being here was to have a good time. You're not gonna look around the room for one more thing to be offended by. And you're not gonna log on to social media to trash a random stranger for the road. No, if anything, you're gonna wish you had a few more of those moments of isolated joy where you're laughing yourself senseless, with no regard for who agrees with your punch line.

For far too long, the outrage mob has thrived by pressuring people into playing along with the pretend notion that we're all supposed to have the same tastes. But we all know that couldn't be any further from the truth.

Online speech is no different from online porn in that it has a million niche audiences and the words people say don't really matter. Sure, there are moments when we all want to wash someone's mouth out with soap, but there are probably videos out there of people doing that too.

Do people say offensive things? Yes.

Has amping up the power that words have over our lives improved anything for literally anyone? No.

Streets aren't safer. Schools aren't smarter. Economies aren't better. And people aren't happier. One of the main reasons why is we're all exhausted from having a law firm on call in our heads twenty-four hours a day to vet every word that comes out of our mouths.

Whether intentional or not, the cancel craze has spawned a war on fun. Millions of people now police comedy, music, movies, and mascots with more intensity than they police our streets. Dead presidents are having their statues pulled down and their names taken off libraries at a time when a third of our schoolkids can't read the books *in* the library. They say Nero fiddled while Rome burned, but if he were alive today, he'd be canceling things instead. It's the same level of detached indifference to the real fires burning in our world.

I don't doubt there are millions of people who disagree with me about whether we need to police speech more intensely. That's fine, because as a wise man once said, "To each his own." Sadly, that wise man would get fired today for gendering that statement, but the dude was right.

In the end, freedom of speech is freedom of fun. And that's why these censorship armies need to be crushed at all costs. They're not a movement of progress. They're a movement of power. They get it by waging a war on fun.

We can't let these losers win.

Acknowledgments

This book would not be possible without my incredible family. To be clear, they contributed *nothing* to the writing process. If anything, they were far too noisy whenever I tried to work at home. But my drive to provide a halfway decent life for these maniacs has me going a lot harder than I ever would for myself. Seriously. Were it not for Jenny and the Linc man, I'd be nothing more than a chubby comedian who spends way too much money on whiskey and cigars. But because of them, I'm a chubby comedian with a nationally syndicated talk show who spends way too much money on whiskey and cigars. Raising one finger to tater tot quiches, convertible Mustangs, and the Jackson 3! Shut up, Daisy, I just fed you.

I'd also like to thank my entire Fox family, but especially the incomparable Suzanne Scott, who makes me proud to work at Fox every day, and Jay Wallace, who's as top-shelf as it gets. Please know I'm eternally grateful to both of you for all the incredible opportunities I've been given, even if I don't always dress like it on the air.

Megan Albano and Meade Cooper should also come up and light a candle at this sweet sixteen for kicking ass every day in every way. Ditto for Lauren Petterson, who's been lights-out from word one.

Yuge shout-out to the Fox News audio team, led by the great John Sylvester. Thank you for giving a regular guy like me a chance and a million laughs to go with it. Mr. Leonard would be proud!

Marvelous Maria Donovan is another hero for managing to keep this cabbie on the radio road every day, no matter how many times I hit the rumble strips.

Okay, let's get to the big-time TV talent before their massive egos throw a fit. . . .

I'll start by thanking Dana Perino for being the gold standard who models excellence for all of us every day. I treasure your friendship, your wit, and your wisdom more than you'll ever know. I was going to apologize for all the dirty jokes in here, but then it dawned on me that Peter has probably told *way* worse.

Sean Hannity has helped me in too many ways to list, so I'll simply say thank you for being one of the coolest, most generous people I'll ever meet. The fact that I get to do your show every week is something I never could have dreamed of when I was a cabdriver. Heck, back then I couldn't have even fathomed getting *tickets* to your show, and here I am now, scalping them outside the studio.

Yuge thanks to Brian Brenberg for being a first-ballot hall of fame friend. I should also mention that Jenny considers you and Krista to be the most well-behaved Fox guests in the history of our backyard, although the bar is *really* low.

Speaking of bars, this whole Fox party couldn't have happened without the cultural icon we call Kennedy. Thank you, from the bottom of my cholesterol-filled heart, for giving me my start in TV and several other areas that can't be mentioned for legal reasons. I'll stop it here, out of respect for our "no compliments" rule.

Brian Kilmeade, you're a world-class guy and a fantastic radio mentor. I just wish you'd work a little harder. Thank you to Alyson, Eric, and Peter for keeping terrestrial radio's reputation in good standing, despite the best efforts of myself and *The Guy Benson Show* to ruin it. (Love you, Guy, Christine, and Dan.)

There are few things in this world I enjoy more than talking to Bill Hemmer on the radio. And on TV you're a first-team all-American who makes every player around you better. If only they had one of you on the Bengals.

Shout-out to Jesse Watters, Johnny B, and the entire prime-time team for always being a hilarious hang. You have no idea how much the Ratings Fairy appreciates all of you, even Tully.

The great Martha MacCallum gets a *giant* gold star for being as cool as they come. It's a true honor to have the friendship of someone as brilliant and badass as you.

Same goes for Shannon Bream, who's an absolute force multiplier of awesomeness wherever she goes.

To the King of Late Night, Greg Gutfeld, and his entire band of merry misfits: I absolutely love every single one of you, no matter how many times you trash the jackets in my "overweight figure skater" collection. Thanks for giving the world a reason to watch late-night comedy again (at least when I'm on).

It's impossible to run into Ainsley Earhardt and not feel better about the world, so thank you for being you, pal.

And a shout-out to Steve Doocy, who always cracks me up, even though his cookbooks are the reason I look like a "before" model in a diet ad.

Janice Dean. You are the best for always being down to "rock and roll" no matter what the forecast calls for. See what I did there, buddy?

Double fist bump for Carley Shimkus and Todd Piro. Most people would *never* book a dude like me on a 5 a.m. TV show because they wouldn't expect him to wake up on time. But you two had the good sense to realize that I'm usually still out from the night before. Well played.

Laura Ingraham and the entire "What the Failla?" crew have been aces from the second I walked into their cable news casino, so thanks for having a girl.

Stuart Varney, you are hilarious and I love doing your show every week, although I'm still convinced you're faking the accent.

Neil Cavuto is a national treasure. I've learned so much from working with you that I probably owe tuition, although we are living in a time of "student loan forgiveness," so please settle for this shout-out.

Katie Pavlich is as cool as they come, and I'm not just saying that because you're probably armed as you read this.

Harris Faulkner deserves a gold medal for having me on her show at 11 a.m., even though I talk like it's 11 p.m. Your support has meant a ton over the years, so *thanks*, Queen of Daytime.

I also need to thank Sean Duffy and Rachel Campos-Duffy for taking time out from their busy schedule of hoarding children to become fantastic friends.

Dana Blanton: When it comes to watercooler conversations, you are number one in every poll, well beyond the margin of error.

Dagen McDowell has been making me laugh since my cabdriving days, which is saying something because most of those shifts made me want to cry. Thanks for all that you do, man!

Jessica Tarlov is a great friend and a greater broadcaster. Everyone in my radio audience is better off for the reasoned and ridiculous banter we engage in, whether they hate you or . . . hate you. Lots of love from the Faillas, though!

And I'd be remiss if I didn't shout out Paul and Joanne Mauro, who've been great to me over the years. You two truly deserve each other, although I'm not sure if that's a compliment or an insult.

Lastly, the biggest thanks allowable by law to Emily Compagno, who became my "ride or die" homie the second I met her. I truly wish I could clone you, if only because I wouldn't have to feel so bad the next time my family accidentally locks you in our garage. Thanks for always playing good ball, Em. Never, ever forget that "the Autumn Wind is a *Raider*."

The following folks might be behind the scenes but they are *way* ahead of the competition:

Jill Van Why is absolutely wonderful to work with, and the entire wardrobe department deserves hazard pay for putting up with my style choices. Manny, Jenna, and Allison, please take a bow and take a few shots.

Same goes for the legends at H&M—*thank you* for making me feel like a whole new woman every time I leave your chairs!

I should also mention that I owe Victor Emmanuel my life for hiring me at Fox, although many people want to take *his* for doing it. "Oink, oink, my good man."

Brett Zoeller, Amy Fenton, and the entire crew on *The Five* deserve a ticker-tape parade for all the incredible work they do. But, alas, New York City has enough debris on the sidewalks, so let's not add more.

On the radio side of town, Rey Erney, Tamara Karcev, David Manning, Willie Sanchez, and Nicole Rabon are all world-class. Same goes for Frank Bruno, Harry Kapsalis, Matt Dahl, Tom Root, and Greg Yock. And it goes without saying that Josh Harman and Mike Addvensky deserve a Gatorade bath for making *Fox Across America* the team nobody wants to play. After all, what's one more spill in the control room at this point?

Maryam Jiminez, Bud Knapp, John Case, Olivia Garner, Sal Foglio, Ashley Serriani, and the entire Fox Nation crew have crushed everything we've worked on. Let the record show that after one standup special and two documentaries, I believe in *all of you* a lot more than the moon landing.

Lynn Jordal Martin and the opinion team are heroes for putting up with my writing on *Dot Com*. Can't thank you enough for the confidence you've shown in this community college grad.

Luke Bozich and Daniel Schmertz keep on crushing this gig like a beer can, and not just because I look like someone who gets paid in Coors Lights.

Big thanks to Chris Mazzilli, Sean Flynn, Andrew Schwartzol, Ed Cavanaugh, and the entire Gotham gang for being the best comedy club on the planet.

Shout-out to William Rodriguez for sending me to all the best theaters, and to Connor Smith and the media relations team for signing my permission slips.

I wish I could individually thank all 155 radio stations that carry *Fox Across America*, but the Oscars orchestra is already starting to play me off the stage. Let's just have a group hug and allow me to thank all of you for having excellent taste in radio.

Lastly, I would like to thank my partner in crime, Dean Imperial, for being the most trusted voice in the huddle for twenty-two years. Can't wait to find a name for whatever diet this book puts me on next.

Ryan Reiss and Charles McBee also belong on "the list" along with my creative kingpins, Sean Barry and Paul Grassini.

And I can't forget my family, try as I might:

Thank you to my mom, Marianne Failla. Dave and Judy Steinke, Smoking Joe Failla, Mike Failla, Joey Failla, Sue Failla, Terri, Michelle, Dan, Dave, Aunt Fran, and always Uncle Sonny. Shout-out to all the other Parillos, Bordinkos, Kokovskis, Steinkes, and Crafts, who make me what I am (a mess).

Finally, thanks to the entire HarperCollins crew, especially Eric Nelson, who edited my coach-class ramblings into a first-class book. And to Lisa Sharkey, who had the courage and the creative flare to attack this cancel craze head-on. Milan Bozic nailed the jacket design, and David Koral somehow made it through the copyedits without quitting the business. Take a bow, you guys!

Lastly, *you*, the reader, cannot be thanked enough for supporting my efforts in TV, radio, and ridiculousness.

If we're ever going to save this country, we don't need more Republicans or more Democrats, we just need less assholes. Thank you for helping me spread my feel-good gospel every day.

All right, folks, the ride is officially over.

Pay up and get the fuck out!

About the Author

Jimmy Failla is a comedian, radio host, TV contributor, and trophy husband. His nationally syndicated talk show, *Fox Across America*, can be heard on more than 150 radio stations, *Fox Nation*, and the Fox News app. He lives on Long Island, New York, with his wife, Jen, and his son, Lincoln. When he's not opiating the masses with his wit and wisdom, he's gambling on youth sports or bottoming out in his backyard with a rotating cast of showbiz figures.